IMP

This illustration by longtime comrade Carlo de Fornaro depicts Ben as Gautama in the poem "The Shrine in the Mist" on page 76.

IMP

the collected poetry of
Benjamin DeCasseres

edited and introduced by
Kevin I. Slaughter

with other writing by
**S. P. Rudens, Don Marquis,
Blanche Shoemaker Wagstaff
& Eugene O'Neill**

*Revised and Expanded
Second Edition*

UNDERWORLD AMUSEMENTS
Baltimore

IMP: The Collected Poetry of Benjamin DeCasseres
ISBN 978-1-943687-40-4 (paperback)

Published by Underworld Amusements
Baltimore, Maryland
WWW.UNDERWORLDAMUSEMENTS.COM

Copyright © 2025 by Kevin I. Slaughter,
compilation, introduction, annotations, and design.
All poems and paratextual elements not by the editor
are in the public domain.

First edition published November 2013.
Revised and expanded second edition issued November 2025.

Cover design by Kevin I. Slaughter and Jeff Bowling.
Bastard title page illustration by Josh Latta:
WWW.LATTALAND.COM

"Introduction" by Kevin I. Slaughter © 2013, revised and
expanded October 2025 as "Shadow-Eater of the Black Suns."

IMP is the second in a series of books collecting
and reviving the writings of Benjamin DeCasseres.
Further information available at:
WWW.BENJAMINDECASSERES.COM

Benjamin DeCasseres is a subject
of study for the Union of Egoists:
WWW.UNIONOFEGOISTS.COM

The Juggernaut

Benjamin DeCasseres is going to begin the weekly publication of a leaflet called *The Juggernaut*. This leaflet will not be for sale. It will live without circulation or advertising. It will, in fact, not be printed on paper or any other material substance.

The Juggernaut will be the unique publication of all time. It will issue every Saturday from the 100-cylinder, 70,000-horsepower brain press of Benjamin DeCasseres. Its leaves will be the sensibility of its author. Its type will be set up by the gods on the Mergenthalers of his multi-moods.

It will be read by Puck, Medusa, Satan, Apollo, Ariel, Hamlet, Don Quixote and the ghosts of all the dead thinkers and poets and fantastics who make a reading room of the soul of Benjamin DeCasseres. It will be what the *Mercure de France*, *La Vie Parisienne*, *Life*, the *Smart Set*, *Vanity Fair*, *Much Ado*, the *Egoist* and *Le Revue des Deux Mondes* would be if they could get along without the shackles of the business office, the man-in-the-subway and the printers' bills.

The Juggernaut, DeCasseres says, will circulate in four dimensions. It will pass all censors. It will defy all codes, bonds, conventions and socialistic-capitalistic theories. Its motto will be:

Be Hard—Live Dangerously.

Jack Cuse
July, 1918

To Benjamin DeCasseres

Stand steady a moment.
Lift me up on your shoulder.
I want to reach up to find if Saturn's rings will burn me.

Ernest M. Hunt

---

*   *The Quill*, November 1919.

In an Old-Time Tavern Booth

To Ben DeCasseres

Drinking, I doze, and see the gods go by;
They wave to me the hand of comradeship,
For I am one with them, and at my lip
The cup of wisdom bubbles up the sky
A blur of moondust drifts to dull mine eye,
But through the veil my romping visions slip
To dance among the careless stars, outstrip
The racing planets where they swoop and fly,

And then—from somewhere east of Mars a keen
Thin wind whines for a Dime; I drop one in
A sad Salvation Army tambourine
And hear a weary homily on Sin—
"Sister," I say, "you're right, and yet the Truth
 Sometimes sits near me in this tavern booth."

Don Marquis

---

* *The Old Soak: and, Hail and Farewell*, New York: Doubleday, Page & Company, 1921.

Benjamin DeCasseres (photographer and date unknown).

Contents

The Juggernaut *"Jack Cuse"* · 5
To Benjamin DeCasseres *Ernest M. Hunt* · · · · · · · · · · · · 6
In an Old-Time Tavern Booth *Don Marquis* · · · · · · · · · · · 7
Shadow-Eater of the Black Suns *Kevin I. Slaughter* · · · · · · · 15
A Fourth Dimensional Mind *S. P. Rudens* · · · · · · · · · · · · 45
Benjamin DeCasseres *Blanche Shoemaker Wagstaff* · · · · · · · 51
Don Marquis · 56
Foreword (to *Anathema!*) *Eugene O'Neill* · · · · · · · · · · · 59
Robinson Jeffers: Tragic Terror · · · · · · · · · · · · · · · · · · 62

THE SHADOW-EATER (1915 & 1923)

The Protagonist · 73
Tantara! Tantaro! · 74
The Tongueless One · 75
The Shrine in the Mist · 76
My Comic Perspective · 77
The Peeper · 78
The-Circle-That-Looks-Like-A-Line · · · · · · · · · · · · · · · · 79
My Divine Hate · 80
The Rotted Ideal · 81
The Vision Malefic · 82
Dying · 84
The Dead Who Live · 85
Exvolved · 86
The God of Negation · 87
Godward · 88
Beyond Sense · 89
The Cynic of Nazareth · 90
De Profundis · 91
On a Marriage · 92
The Syncopated Spinner · 93
Love and Sleep · 94
The Watcher · 95
Face to Face · 96
My Shadows · 97

The Vigil · 98
The Closed Room · 99
Half-Seen · 100
The Long Vigil · 101
Prophetic · 102
Resurrection Night · 103
Bird of The Night · 104
The Cleft In The Wall · 105
The Truant · 106
Change and an Ending · 107
The Quest in the Flesh · 108
In the Adytum · 109
The Way Out: Bio · 110
Moth-Terror · 111
My Holy Lust · 112
The Overone · 113
The Ultimate · 114
The Sleeper · 115
The Alleys of Eld · 116
Love the Destroyer · 117
Rejection · 118
The Spear of the Great Spurning · · · · · · · · · · · · 119

SUBLIME BOY (1926)

Resolved · 121
Uprendered · 123
Unwithered · 124
Waiting · 126
Pre-Destined · 127
Home · 128
Immune · 129

ANATHEMA! LITANIES OF NEGATION (1928)

Anathema! Litanies of Negation · · · · · · · · · · · · · · 133

BLACK SUNS (1936)

The Overlord · 159
Walter · 160

The Decoy · 161
The Haunted House · 162
Marche Funebre · 163
Chimeras · 164
Magical Night · 165
Fantasia · 166
In the Backyard of Life · 167
Man · 168
Shelley · 169
Imagination · 170
Keats · 171
Facts · 172
The Tragic Bluffer · 174
The Humorist · 175
Dawn · 176
Sleep · 177
The Pickpocket · 178
Vers Libre · 179
A Son of God · 181
The Ideal · 182
Miracles · 183
Sea-Mania · 184
Strayling · 185
Ave, Zarathustra! · 186
The Thief · 187
Swinburne · 188
The Vat · 189
Masque of the Minutes · 190
Salutation · 197
Ingression · 198

UNCOLLECTED, VARIATIONS, & TRANSLATIONS (1897–1945)

Sorrow's Balm · 203
The Wisdom of Gautama · · · · · · · · · · · · · · · · · · 204
Prayer · 205
Solitude · 206
Solitude · 207

West Point	208
Revelation	209
Late Autumn	210
An Incident	211
In the Slums	212
My Lamp	213
Bio	214
The Gallic Lark and the Sow-on-the Rhine	215
L'alouette Gauloise Et La Truie Du Rhin	216
Pater Noster	217
Pater Noster	219
Pater Noster	221
To Emile Verhaeren	223
The Haunted House	224
The Mysterious Weaver	225
Potporri	226
W.S.: 1616–1916	227
The Hague—1915	228
Night Cometh	229
Song of Songs	230
The Humorist	231
Birth of a Sword	232
Across the Gulf	233
The Conquerors	234
In the Ramble	236
Fifty!	237
The Pacifist's Breviary	238
Nocturne	239
On Coney's Beach	240
"Let Us Have Peace"	241
Morning Magic	242
Chatterton	243
The Inevitable	244
Ruins	245
The Masses	246
Harlequin's Confession	247
My Golden Age	248
The Risen Giant!	249

The Poet-Burglar	250
Sleep	251
March Winds	252
Sub Specie Eternitatis	253
The Eternal Avatar	254
Chant of Man, 1917	255
The Soul of It All	256
Similes and a Query	257
Letter-Boxes	258
Hold Yet a Little While!	259
Variations on an Old Theme	260
[untitled]	261
The Lady of the Hour	262
German Pronouns	263
Birth Mannerisms	264
The Vampire	265
To a Great American	266
Credo for Eunuch-Pacifists	267
Anarch	268
Arise, Ye Dead!	269
Italy	270
The Ball Game	271
The Muses of the Moment	272
Foch!	273
D'Annunzio	274
The Eter-Null	275
"Progress"	276
Wind	277
The Dream Pocket	278
Fantasie	279
Vicariously	280
New York	281
Nocturne: 1920	282
Threshold	283
The Sea	284
Rum's 7 Cardinal Virtues	285
Fermentation	286
Vision	287

The Poet and the Hooligans ·················· 288
Peter Pan ································ 289
To the Old Soak ·························· 290
Jugement ······························· 291
The Bootlegger's Daughter ················· 292
Prélude ································· 293
L'aiguillon dans la Chair ···················· 297
Rejet ··································· 298
Ma Passion Sacrée ······················· 299
Codpiece ······························· 300
Le Dormeur ····························· 301
Litanies de la Négation ····················· 302
The Presence: Hymn of a Nihilist to Oblivion ·········· 303

Poet Nears Delectable State ················ 305
Index ································· 310

Shadow-Eater of the Black Suns
Kevin I. Slaughter

Benjamin DeCasseres (1873–1945) was one of the most prolific and unruly American men of letters in the early twentieth century. A writer without boundaries, he moved fluidly among journalism, poetry, satire, polemics, aphorism, and plays. His restless energy and taste for provocation made him a fixture in both mainstream and avant-garde circles, though he never entirely belonged to either. He worked on the first American release of the silent film classic *Nosferatu*—credited in some film histories with writing the English intertitles—and wrote regular criticism, trade-journal essays, and reviews for *Motion Picture Herald* and other film magazines during the 1920s and 1930s. He even arranged to take—and be filmed drinking—the first legal glass of alcohol after the repeal of Prohibition in 1933, a publicity gesture as theatrical as his prose.

DeCasseres' career was astonishingly varied. In 1906–1907, he lived in Mexico City, editing the English-language edition of *El Diario,* and appearing in translation in the Spanish-language editions, thus entering that country's cosmopolitan journalistic world. Earlier still, he had collaborated with Elbert Hubbard, and even ghostwrote for him, contributing to Hubbard's *Philistine* and *Fra* magazines. In New York, he ran for mayor in 1913 as a self-proclaimed "Cubist candidate," a flamboyant act of aesthetic politics aligning him with the city's modernist and bohemian currents. Around the same time, he was loosely associated with Alfred Stieglitz's *Camera Work* circle, part of a generation of writers and critics bridging visual art and literature. Contemporary accounts by DeCasseres himself in *The American Mercury* ("Joel's," 1932; "Jack's," 1932) leave no doubt that he was among the habitués of New York's pre-Prohibition café culture. In his memoir of Joel Rinaldo's Bohemia, he recalls the "Literary and Revolutionary Table—Reserved for Literature and Revolution," where he and figures such as Carlo de Fornaro, Sadakichi Hartmann, Michael Monahan, Hippolyte Havel, Emma Goldman, and even Leon Trotsky, gathered over *chili con carne* and "scuttles of beer".

DeCasseres wrote across decades of upheaval: two world wars, the Russian Revolution, the rise and fall of fascism, the Great Depression, and the American experiment with Prohibition. His writing bristled with defiance in this tumultuous context, blending Nietzschean individualism, cosmic pessimism, and a distinctly American bravado. He was among the earliest American popularizers of Nietzsche and Stirner, frequently name-dropping them and writing essays that helped introduce their ideas to a broader public. He championed the sovereignty of the self against gods, governments, and traditions alike, yet his iconoclasm was never doctrinaire; he could be found in anarchist journals like Hippolyte Havel's *Revolt*, Laurance Labadie's *Discussion* and E. Armand's *L'En Dehors*, but also in the pages of *The New York Sun* or *Cosmopolitan*. In all these venues, he wrote with the same forceful conviction that the universe was a stage for revolt, mockery, and myth-making.

If his journalism made him widely read, it was his poetry that revealed the full reach of his imagination. DeCasseres' verse spans youthful experiments in hymn-like forms to apocalyptic litanies of negation, from the venomous outpouring of *The Shadow-Eater* to the surreal cosmic visions of *Black Suns*. He frequently cast himself in mythic terms—Vulcan, Satan, the Anarch—while simultaneously undermining his own grandeur with irony. His poetic voice fused Symbolist decadence with American irreverence, often anticipating themes later associated with existentialism and surrealism.

Despite his remarkable output, DeCasseres remains a neglected figure. No full biography has yet been written, and, until my efforts began in 2012, his works survived largely in out-of-print volumes, pamphlets, and periodicals. Yet his contemporaries recognized his significance: Eugene O'Neill contributed a foreword to his book-length poem *Anathema!*, Don Marquis prefaced *The Shadow-Eater*, and his writings were translated—however minimally—into Sapnish, French, Romanian, and Japanese during his lifetime. He was an early expositor of Nietzsche and Stirner in America, and his Francophilia brought him into dialogue with Symbolists and anarchists abroad. In many ways, he lived and wrote as a bridge between worlds: between journalism and literature, between satire and metaphysics, between Old World decadence and New World spectacle.

The poems in this volume must be read with an awareness of these tensions. They belong to an age when modern art was dismantling tradition—when *vers libre*, Cubism, and Dada opened new terrains of form and thought—and yet they are also deeply personal eruptions, what DeCasseres himself called his "Gargantuan evacuation of venom, lava and contempt." Here we find not only a record of an age of extremes, but the voice of a man who insisted on being extreme in it.

In assembling DeCasseres' collected poetry, one faces a choice in approach to collecting the poetry of one writer. The first is selective: to extract the finest work and discard the weaker verses, recognizing that even great poets are uneven. The second is archival: to preserve everything that can be called a poem, regardless of merit. This volume largely follows the latter approach, with some caveats expounded upon at the end of this introduction.

The last line of the first edition of this volume promised: "I expect that one day an expanded edition of *IMP* will appear with even more lost works." That day has arrived—twelve years later. Yet as with DeCasseres himself, whose writings continue to surface in forgotten magazines and neglected archives, the work will reveal itself to be unfinished. More poems will undoubtedly emerge, each one another facet of a voice at once prophetic, blasphemous, comic, and sublime. May enough rise up to issue a future revision.

Introductory Materials

The prefatory material helps situate Benjamin DeCasseres not only as a solitary iconoclast, but also as a figure who moved in significant literary and artistic circles. Each contribution reflects how contemporaries perceived him: as friend, provocateur, or visionary.

The section opens with "The Juggernaut" (pg. 5), signed "Jack Cuse." The pseudonym is a play on the French *j'accuse* ("I accuse")—a bitter denunciation—and it is almost certainly DeCasseres writing in his own voice under a mask. This kind of self-mythologizing gesture was typical of him: he used pseudonyms and staged his identity in the third person, mixing seriousness with irony. What begins as a note of introduction is in fact a declaration of revolt, a clue to the way DeCasseres wished his poetry to be received.

Following this are two tributes from friends. Ernest M. Hunt's short poem "To Benjamin DeCasseres" (pg. 6), and Don Marquis' "In an Old-Time Tavern Booth" (pg. 7) offer affectionate portrayals of the man behind the work.

After my own introduction, I have chosen to reprint a short biographical essay that appeared in the *Reflex* of December, 1927. (pg. 45).

A booklet edition, printed later, states:

> Its author, Mr. S. P. Rudens, is a native of Russia and graduated from the University of Chicago in 1915. He has been a teacher of English and mathematics, was managing editor of *East and West*, an associate editor of the *Chicago Literary Times* with Ben Hecht and Maxwell Bodenheim, and is now assistant director of the Jewish People's Institute of Chicago. He has translated many volumes of plays and poems from the German and Yiddish, and is the author of over two hundred essays in criticism and of general articles.
>
> Mr. Rudens says: "Criticism implies and requires as passionate an affirmation of one's personality and of life as any other form of art."

Blanche Shoemaker Wagstaff's essay "Benjamin DeCasseres," (pg. 51) reprinted from *The Poetry Journal* in 1915, shows how his reputation had already crossed into more formal literary venues. Wagstaff was herself a New York poet of some note, and her recognition of DeCasseres placed him in the company of writers being actively promoted to readers of serious poetry. That same issue reprinted two poems from *The Shadow-Eater*, giving them circulation among audiences that might otherwise never have encountered his work.

Don Marquis, remembered today for *Archy and Mehitabel*, was one of DeCasseres' closest literary allies. His "Preface" (pg. 55) to the third edition of *The Shadow-Eater* situates DeCasseres within the ferment of early modern American literature, affirming both the shock and the necessity of his voice. That Marquis—himself a popular humorist with a wide readership—chose to stand as DeCasseres' advocate speaks volumes about how seriously he regarded his friend's artistic contribution. DeCasseres' later eulogy for Marquis, included here, closes the circle of his friendship with a tone of mournful respect.

Next it is Eugene O'Neill's foreword to *Anathema!*, (pg. 59) DeCasseres' epic "Satanic poem." O'Neill, who would go on to win the Nobel Prize in Literature, recognized in DeCasseres a writer of uncompromising intensity. His willingness to lend his name to so incendiary a work indicates the esteem he held for DeCasseres' fearless imagination.

Although the final prefatory text is ostensibly about another poet, "Robinson Jeffers: Tragic Terror" (pg. 62) deserves inclusion in this volume because it is simultaneously a vivid piece of DeCasseresian criticism and a revealing self-portrait. In praising Jeffers's fatalism, aesthetic severity, and Dionysian mysticism, Benjamin DeCasseres highlights precisely those qualities that mirror his own artistic temperament. His essay reads not only as an appreciation of Jeffers's verse, but as an oblique declaration of DeCasseres' own tragic metaphysics and poetic ideals.

Taken together, these introductory writings reveal the paradox of Benjamin DeCasseres' position: he was both marginal and central. Marginal in the sense that his books were often privately printed, his audience small, and his outlook too corrosive for mainstream taste. Yet central in that major figures—Marquis, O'Neill, Steiglitz, and later Ayn Rand—were willing to align themselves with him, testifying that his voice mattered in the literary conversation of his time. These documents preserve not only the context for the poems that follow, but also the testimony of those who recognized in him a rare, if difficult, talent.

The Shadow-Eater (1915 / 1917 / 1923)

If one book secured Benjamin DeCasseres' reputation as a poet, it was *The Shadow-Eater*. First published in 1915 by Albert & Charles Boni, it comprised 46 poems written between 1902 and 1906. The first edition featuring a frontispiece portrait by Marius de Zayas was limited to 650 copies, of which 150 were printed on Tuscany handmade paper, included a tipped in frontispiece portrait of the author by Marius de Zayas (that would reappear in the 1923 edition) and signed by the author.

The book as a whole and specifically the first poem is dedicated to author and illustrator Carlo de Fornaro. It reads:

> These poems are dedicated to
> CARLO DE FORNARO
> who was the first to understand,
> appreciate and sympathize with them

After moving back to the United States, with DeCasseres' help, De Fornaro wrote a book critical of the Mexican president and others in power, and was eventually found guilty of libel and sentenced to a year of hard labor.

In his quasi-diary *Fantasia Impromptu*, DeCasseres wrote about *The Shadow-Eater* and his writing:

I have tossed out my books helter-skelter. I have written poems and essays without any conscious knowledge of "theme." But they possessed a unity profounder than I knew. In the years of unwitting creation I found I had been making poems and books that fell into ordered wholes and mass-themes. There were group-ideas and linked super-reasonings and themes of which I was never conscious until I began to grope around to arrange them for publication.

Thus all the poems in *The Shadow-Eater*—tossed into a drawer as they were written as if my hand were a planchette on a Ouija board—I found linked by one theme: the ever lasting protest of Man against the brutality of "the gods."

Elsewhere he wrote:

The Shadow-Eater was my great gesture of revolt. It was my Gargantuan evacuation of venom, lava and contempt. It was my ego vomiting itself over worlds, gods, Gods, men and forms. Then came indifference, serenity, calm—the passage to Epicurus and Spinoza and Whitman. Followed by another distention of hate and spleen and cosmic fury embodied in *Anathema!*

A second printing appeared in 1917 from Wilmarth Publishing; this edition is substantially identical to the 1915 Boni edition in content, differing mainly in publisher and date, and including the same set of 46 poems.

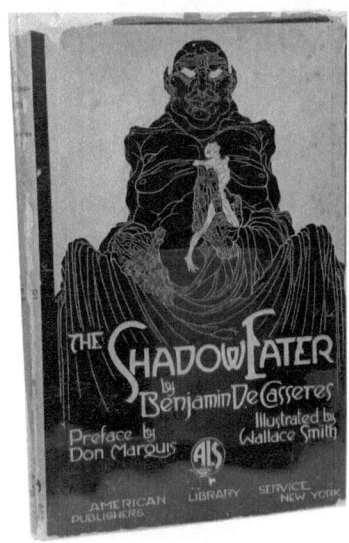

One unimpressed reviewer for *The Dial* commented on "sighings and shriekings of such a Neo-Nietzschean as Benjamin De Casseres," further stating "he seems to take a morbid joy in the leering of lean and filthy specters. Far from seeing the world in a grain of sand, he readily reduces it to a pebble in his shoe. He appears to be on more intimate terms with pain than with poetry, and his attempt to relieve his

"The Dead Who Live" by Wallace Smith.

agonies by screaming in uppercase letters is more to be pitied than encouraged."

In 1923, a revised edition was published by the American Library Service. This version retains almost all the poems except "Love the Destroyer" (pg. 117). It also introduces new visual and paratextual elements: a preface by Don Marquis, reintroduction of the frontispiece portrait by Marius de Zayas, and Wallace Smith illustrated the cover, a plate for the front board, and created a full page illustration for the poem "The Dead Who Live" (pg. 85). Minor revisions to wording, line-breaks, punctuation, and typographical details are scattered through many poems.

The typesetting of the poems varies from the first and second editions, sometimes significantly, as in a whole line missing from "In the Adytum" (pg. 81), noted at the foot of the page.

In "The Shrine in the Mist" (pg. 76) there are a few changes of note. In the first stanza, the line originally read "...mockeries of the fiends that I know—that I know?—". Later, the word "belly" was changed to "guts," "leer" was replaced with "glass," and lastly "mists" with "pulp."

"My Shadows" (pg. 97) had the word "pain-griddles" changed to "pain-ladders", whereas "Change and Ending" has "sick-yellowed" flipped to "yellow-sick".

The most remarkable difference in the second edition is the complete extrication of the poem "Love the Destroyer" (pg. 117). Again, it's speculative, but when the first edition was printed, DeCasseres and his great love Adele "Bio" DeCasseres (born Adella Mary Terrill; formerly Jones) were separated and in the process of a 16-year letter-writing exchange (see his *Love Letters of a Living Poet*, 1931). They were finally reunited in 1919 and shortly thereafter were married.

I have generally used the styling of the third edition. A handwritten note in a copy in my personal collection, dated March 1926, states "(These poems) were begun in 1902, so you will note they antedate all the poetry of today." Indeed, after the last poem the collection is signed off "NEW YORK CITY, 1902-1906."

The Sublime Boy (1926)

The Sublime Boy vies with *Love Letters of a Living Poet* as being the most personal volume connected to Benjamin DeCasseres. Compiled after the suicide of his younger brother Walter at the age of eighteen, the book is both a memorial and a collaboration across death. Benjamin salvaged Walter's verses from scraps and fragments, arranging them into a slim volume. Yet he did not stop there: he appended several of his own poems, elegiac pieces that meditate on mortality, beauty, and visionary loss.

In doing so, DeCasseres turned *The Sublime Boy* into something more than a tribute; it became a dialogue between brothers, one silenced prematurely, the other wrestling with grief. The book reveals a tender dimension often obscured by Benjamin's more volcanic or satirical writings. Here his philosophy of revolt is tempered by intimacy, as he struggles not against gods or fate in the abstract, but against death's personal theft. In tone and subject, *The Sublime Boy* anticipates later works like "Ruins" and "My Golden Age," where he directly confronts his own legacy.

Once published, DeCasseres sent a copy to his friend Robinson Jeffers, and its delayed reception ended up corresponding with the suicide of their mutual friend and poet George Sterling:*

November 16, 1926

Dear Ben:

The book of your brother's poems was delayed in the mail—returned for postage—and has been here only a couple of days, while I've been thinking what to write to you. I can't believe that comment of mine could be of importance one way or the other. My literary judgments are narrow, perhaps, and never

---

* Robin Jeffers to Benjamin De Casseres, November 16–17, 1926, in Ann N. Ridgeway, *The Letters of Robinson Jeffers: A Record of Four Friendships* (Ph.D. diss., Bowling Green State University, 1966), 155–156

enthusiastic; I wish they were, in this case. I'd give a lot to be able to say something splendid.

But in the first place, I can't go along with your brilliantly written preface. Suicide is often justifiable, very rarely admirable. As a rejection of life it is only justifiable; you can't praise a man for going to bed early.

And there was much to praise in your brother. There was talent that might have developed transcendently; it is simply impossible to foretell a boy's manhood. If Chatterton had lived he might have been the greatest English poet; he might have gone silent like Rimbaud; he might have dwindled into mediocrity.

Walter DeCasseres had splendid possibilities; he refused life, as he had a right to do, and all that you have is a shining memory, and these brief sweet-blooded poems to share with us. They are musical, clear and sweet; often they rise to a faint impersonal ecstasy as in the haunting line "A shadow worshipped and a shadow worshipper"; once at least, in "The Suicide," to a bare bitter earnestness that captures beauty because it does not want beauty.

Thank you for having the book sent to me. Indeed I wish I could speak more fluently about it.

November 17

I wrote this last night and kept it over the day wondering how it could be bettered. To-day came the tragic news of George (Sterling)'s death. I haven't the heart to rewrite to-night, and I mustn't delay this answer longer. It appears from the paper that a bottle of poison was found uncorked in George's room; ironical that I should have been writing that cold paragraph about suicide last night. You and I have lost a great friend, there was none more generous or more constant. It seems incredible that we'll have neither letter nor visit from him.

Yours,
Robin Jeffers

Anathema! Litanies of Negation (1928)

If *The Shadow-Eater* was DeCasseres' great act of defiance, *Anathema!* was its darker sequel: a vast blasphemous litany that magnified his revolt to cosmic proportions. Published in 1928 by Gotham Book Mart in 1,250 signed copies, it was introduced by Eugene O'Neill. O'Neill called it "far more than a hymn of renunciation. It is the torment and ecstasy of a mystic's questioning of life," recognizing that DeCasseres' thunderous "No" to gods and creeds carried within it a paradoxical affirmation of the chaos and truth in man's soul.

Structured as fifty-five litanies, the work is a sustained chant of negation. Gods, kings, moral codes, and the very machinery of existence are invoked only to be cursed, mocked, and cast down. Its voice is both biblical and anti-biblical, borrowing the grandeur of liturgy only to reverse it into a hymn of damnation. Where *The Shadow-Eater* revealed personal spleen, *Anathema!* aspires to universal indictment. The influence of Nietzsche and Stirner is unmistakable, refracted through DeCasseres' flamboyant American idiom, while its grotesque and exalted imagery recalls Comte de Lautréamont's *Les Chants de Maldoror*. The poem stages rebellion as spectacle: Satan becomes not a tempter, but a hero of defiance; humanity's cries become choruses of cosmic laughter. In this sense, *Anathema!* anticipates later writers like Antonin Artaud and Georges Bataille, who likewise sought to turn philosophy into ritual and language into ordeal.

In 1930, DeCasseres inscribed a copy of *Anathema!* to Silas Newton[*] with the words:

> I consider this my greatest production, certainly my highest flight, written during the first year of the mental and spiritual stress of the Great War.

Contemporaries struggled to digest it. *The Bookman* described reading DeCasseres as "to apply an electric drill"—invigorating

---

[*] Silas M. Newton (1887–1972) was a Texas oilman and private-press patron who in 1930 published Benjamin DeCasseres' *Mencken & Shaw* under his own imprint. He later gained notoriety for his part in the so-called "Aztec UFO crash" hoax of 1948, one of the earliest and most publicized flying-saucer stories in the United States.

but fatiguing. The *Saturday Review of Literature* called him "a passionate, erratic poet [who] strives to shake the foundation of the world," while *The Nation* observed that he "occupies a niche that is all his own." Even the *New York Times* admitted, "There is but one Benjamin DeCasseres... to read him is to experience the greatest mental exhilaration."

Finally, I quote John G. Neihardt from the November 30, 1928 edition of *St. Louis Post-Dispatch*:

> This, it will be noted, is simply the ancient satanic gospel of despair, as variously preached by Lucretius, Leopardi, Schopenhauer, Nietzsche and many others in many ages; and it is doubtful if it has ever been expressed more effectively than in this mad rhapsody.

Black Suns (1936)

Again, from his *Fantasia Impromptu*:

> Sometimes whole poems would blaze forth in the sky of my brain and I would leap from my bed to my table and

put them down. I have made very few changes in them, either in *The Shadow-Eater, Anathema!* or *Black Suns*. I never planned a poem or sat down in a cold waking state "to write a poem" in my life. They were forged in the black chambers of Sleep by a mysterious Blacksmith.

Black Suns was printed in 1936 as part of a series of 23 self-published paperback booklets that were eventually collected into a three volume set published as *The Works of Benjamin DeCasseres* in an edition of 25 copies. The short description at the beginning stated that it was only the first half of the entire book, and a flyer indicated that "part 2" was to be the 24th book in the series. It is unknown to me why he stopped one booklet short of his announced goal, but other booklets mention they'd continue into volumes well past 24.

"Haunted House" (pg. 162) was first published in a magazine titled *Others* (May-June 1916) in a longer variant that I have located.

"Vers Libre" (pg. 179) appears in the July, 1916 edition of *Current Opinion*, though I'll allow their preface to give framing:

> If we are not mistaken, Benjamin DeCasseres is the first artist of the "new poetry" to explain *vers libre* in "Vers Libre." Recently he contributed a poem to Don Marquis's column of humor in the *New York Evening Sun* which that talented snapper-up of bright trifles declares the best thing he has read "in the way of an exposition of what the writers of vers libre are (or should be) aiming at.

Since the poems are identical, only the *Black Suns* version is printed here. "Masque of the Minutes" (pg. 190) was, in the first edition of *IMP*, broken out into a separate chapter from the

Black Suns poems, where it first appeared in its final form. There were two previously printed variants that included some textual variations, and slightly different formatting and styling. I have reintegrated the text into *Black Suns* section and typeset it as a single poem.

Uncollected, Variations, & Translations (1897–1945)

This final section gathers poems outside DeCasseres' published collections, including variants, translations produced during his lifetime, and a handful of newly recovered items. They are arranged by date of publication, and demonstrate both the scope of his career and the wide range of venues where his work appeared. In the first edition there were 28 poems in what I then called "Disparate Sources." That number has swelled to 94 in this edition.

Although this edition of *IMP* benefits from the growing accessibility of digitized archives, the recovery of forgotten works still depends on active research rather than chance discovery. Many of DeCasseres' writings remain scattered or poorly indexed, and some—such as *The Aristocrat* (Lynchburg, VA, 1932–1933), a short-lived magazine edited by Lewis Carter Randolph and subtitled "*A Periodical for Superior People*"—have remained virtually undocumented for decades. DeCasseres contributed to its debut issue with a piece defining the term "aristocrat," and at least one subsequent issue (Vol. 1, No. 2) survives today in the Modern Poetry Little Magazine Collection at the University of Chicago. The increasing reach of searchable online repositories makes such discoveries more feasible, but it is the deliberate effort to locate, verify, and preserve these materials that continues to expand the known record of DeCasseres' work.

In this section I have given in to my want to provide framing and context to many of these "lost" poems, and have done so in a way that I have not with the work previously presented. I think that many of them, lacking the original context of time and space, may not have as strong a presence as they would otherwise. Possibly I've overindulged myself, favoring these rediscovered pieces for their obscurity while offering only cursory attention to the works he considered worthy of collection.

The earliest known poem, "Sorrow's Balm" (1897) (pg. 203), predates the previously earliest known "The Wisdom of Gautama" by just over a year. It is a plain poem of grief and consolation, in ABAB quatrains that evoke Methodist hymnody. Only the odd mention of a "Giant's voice" hints at mythic depths. Considering DeCasseres' very early use of *vers libre* and association with Dadaist themes a few years later, it is interesting his career as a youthful poet could have been set to a composition by William Billings and sung in a Sunday school without controversy. "The Wisdom of Gautama" (1898) (pg. 204) is more characteristic, drawing on Eastern mysticism and themes of detachment from desire. Phrases such as "diadems crowned" and "marmorial beauty" already show his precision with language.

A long gap followed, broken only by "Prayer" (pg. 205), a prose-poem published in *Cosmopolitan* (October 1907). Here "prayer" is redefined as any act of discovery or courage: Galileo's telescope, Columbus's ship, Franklin's lightning rod. Widely reprinted in religious newsletters like *The Washington News Letter* (1913), it slipped unnoticed into numerous Christian periodicals despite its radical intent.

"Solitude" (1911) (pg. 206), published in *The Papyrus: A Magazine of Individuality*, is the first clear poetic expression of his Nietzschean individualism, later translated in *Hors du troupeau* (1912) by E. Armand. The period between "The Wisdom of Gautama" and "Solitude" saw him publishing essays on Emerson, D'Annunzio, Schwob, Balzac, Whitman, and Rodin, and appearing in venues as diverse as Stieglitz's *Camera Work*, the occult journal *The Mind*, and the *New York Sun*.

While the first poem appears when Benjamin was 24 years old, and his last after his passing at 72, most of the uncollected poems here date from 1915–1920, though his poetic work extended across his life. Many were scattered in ephemeral publications or left out of collections, suggesting both his selectivity and the instability of his publishing outlets. In *The International* alone he published seven poems, appearing alongside figures as disparate as occultist Aleister Crowley and the anarchist poet and sculptor Adolf Wolff. The magazine's editor, George Sylvester Viereck, was himself a study in contradictions—famous in his time for his charming early poetry, anti-war activism, and high-profile interviews with figures such as the Pope, Einstein, and Mussolini. Today, however, he is remembered infamously for writing what is likely the first homoerotic prison memoir, composed after being jailed as a Nazi spy.

These poems often reflect Benjamin DeCasseres' fusion of Symbolist decadence, Nietzschean introspection, and metaphysical despair. In "Revelation" (pg. 209), he conjures a haunting image of spiritual paralysis through stark repetition and apocalyptic resignation. "An Incident" veers into the surreal, blending eroticism, mysticism, and violence in a ritualistic tableau that collapses beauty into annihilation. "In the Slums" turns inward, mapping a psychological underworld where alienation and guilt fester, far from the "brilliantly lighted avenues" of conscious thought.

Finally "Bio" (pg. 214) is his love-letter to the woman he would marry nearly a decade later, Adella "Bio" DeCasseres (1875–1964).

DeCasseres loved France, and France returned the favor. His poems and essays appeared in *Mercure de France*—the same journal that first published French translations of Nietzsche—and in *L'En Dehors*, E. Armand's individualist anarchist paper. In *The Paris Times* of January 5, 1926, Arthur Moss complained of the bibliographic carelessness of *Navire d'Argent* for omitting "the numerous essays and stories of Benjamin DeCasseres, which appeared in French translation in *Revue des Deux Mondes* and other important Paris publications." Such remarks testify to his profile abroad. When he died, several French newspapers carried notices. This final section of the book includes all known lifetime translations of his poetry, even one for which no English original has been located.

"The Gallic Lark and the Sow-on-the-Rhine" (pg. 215) appears alongside its French translation, "*L'Alouette Gauloise et la Truie du Rhin*" (pg. 216). The wartime poem contrasts the lark, a creative and idealistic symbol of France and the aggressive and envious sow as Germany.

The earliest known printing of the poem is a postcard addressed to Don C. Seitz of *The New York World*, postmarked July 4, 1915

The Gallic Lark and the Sow-on-the Rhine

—*To France in Arms*

THE LARK (*whirling in the azure*):
    I orbit in the suns of my Vision, my heart is the Grail of Life.
    I am France, the Athens of Europe, Dionysiac, singing in strife.

THE SOW-ON-THE-RHINE:
    I am the mother of nations, I am the savior of men,
    I am the Sphinx and Revealer—thou art but a wingèd hen.

THE LARK:
    I sing the Song of the Ages, I sing the song of the free,
    I sang in the heart of Ronsard, and the Voice in the Maid was of me!

THE SOW-ON-THE-RHINE:
    Give me your wings and your lightness, give me your dreams and your Eye—
    I hate thee, I love thee, thou wild bird—come down and live in my sty.

THE LARK:
    O Sow that would be Alborak! O Sow of Elysian dreams!
    Thy sty is the dung-pit of learning, thy snout with Flemish blood gleams.

THE SOW-ON-THE-RHINE:
    Curse thy lilt and thy wild heart, curse the air and the light thou dost cleave!
    Curse the Song thou dost sing to thy Loved Ones, who of thy songs Victory weave!

THE LARK:
    I orbit in the suns of my Vision, my heart is a Grail and an Inn;
    My songs have anealed into iron, old Sow with the helmet of tin!

NEW YORK CITY, 1915.   —*Benjamin De Casseres*

(Times Sq. Sta., NY) and July 5, 1915 A.M. (Cashiers Dep't / Chas. Haas). Seitz was the paper's business manager and a noted journalist. The card, now held by Brown University, likely served to transmit the poem to French readers—and to Rémy de Gourmont, who translated and published it in *Dans la tourmente* (April–July 1915). It was introduced with the line: "*M. Benjamin DeCasseres, le poète américain, nous envoie ce petit poème étrange et enflammé.*" ("Mr. Benjamin DeCasseres, the American poet, sends us this little strange and impassioned poem.") The translation closely follows the original but makes a few notable changes. To note two: "Grail of Life" becomes "*clairon de la vie*" ("clarion of life"), shifting from mystical to martial. "Alborak," a reference to the mythic steed of Muhammad, is omitted. The tone remains intense, but some references are adapted for a French audience. The English-language version of the poem was later reprinted in the *New-York Tribune* on April 23, 1918.

"Pater Noster" (pg. 217) is one of DeCasseres' most incendiary and blasphemous poems, a furious inversion of prayer that indicts divine providence as cosmic sadism. The earliest version I have located is a French translation by Rémy de Gourmont, published in *Mercure de France*. Though DeCasseres was a lifelong Francophile, there is no indication he wrote the piece originally in French; the English version remains lost. Building through a conflagration of rage, the poem invokes mythological and historical figures—Érynnie, Torquemada, Nero—to portray God as torturer, tyrant, and executioner. It ends quoting Racine's *Athalie* in the voice of Joas, the innocent child who proclaims faith in a benevolent deity who feeds even the birds. In DeCasseres' hands, this gentle image becomes a savage mockery of those who cling to consolation in the face of horror.

The poem is prefaced by De Gourmont with the following:

> **God or the Other.**—It happened more than once, during the first centuries of that Christianity which had supposedly renewed the world, that poor peoples, terrified by the course worldly affairs were taking, asked themselves very seriously whether it was not the Devil who governed them, or at least whether he did not share

dominion with God himself. Then, in their fear and prudence, they worshipped both principles, that of good and that of evil. And to better assure themselves of the protection of the Evil One, they began practicing all his works with diabolical zeal, while at other moments they fingered their rosaries before the altars. There was great turmoil in consciences. I would not be much surprised if I were told that Manichaeism has returned in these times we are passing through. Does God still reign as master? Has he not been forced to yield a portion of his power? Perhaps some already ask themselves these blasphemous questions (whose fault is it?), while awaiting the supreme question: Has he been dethroned, and do we not now have Satan himself as our God?—and above all while awaiting consciences, wholly devoted, to answer yes.

Flaubert recounts that his mother, an honest and upright woman, upon suddenly seeing her daughter die—an innocent young bride—at once ceased to believe in God. People will say that this woman lacked theological spirit. No doubt, but for many people the idea of God is confused with the very idea of justice. Conscious of having done no wrong to the All-Powerful, they ask themselves why the All-Powerful and All-Just has struck them brutally with his fist. What would Flaubert's mother have said if she had seen Prussian soldiers enter her house, strip and rape her daughter before her eyes, then disembowel her, then set fire to the house and shoot all the neighbors, then shoot her as well or beat her to death and leave her for dead? She would have dimly felt the same sentiments expressed by an American poet, Benjamin DeCasseres, who set himself up as the judge of God and violently reproached him for the crimes upon which the year 1914 came to its close.

This piece is of such great lyrical movement that I wanted to translate it. Here it is. It recalls certain invectives of *Maldoror*, but the author is not a *Maldoror*; he perhaps does not even know him. He is a poet..."

The poem's afterlife is as remarkable as its content. A Romanian translation (pg. 219) appeared in *Flacăra: literară, artistică, socială* on July 11, 1915, in an article by Dragoș Protopopescu, a Shakespeare scholar and member of the Iron Guard. This translation was based on Gourmont's French version, showing the poem's circuitous transmission through European avant-garde and political circles. It is, to my knowledge, the only non-French translation of DeCasseres' poetry during his lifetime. His notoriety as a blasphemous poet thus reached as far as Bucharest, where it was presented as evidence of the "heresy and degeneracy rampant in the less holy countries."

To complete the triptych of blasphemy, I have included here a new English translation (pg. 221), reconstructed from the French. It can only be approximate, but I have attempted to preserve both the fury of its iconoclasm and the bitter irony of its closing lines.

DeCasseres' poem "To Emile Verhaeren" (pg. 223) is a fervent invocation to the Belgian Symbolist poet, casting him in mythic terms—as Titan, Vulcan, and Dionysian seer—and urging him to transform the horrors of World War I, particularly the atrocities at Aerschot and Louvain, into a poetic "Song of Vengeance and Victory" in the spirit of Victor Hugo's *Les Châtiments*.

"The Mysterious Weaver" (pg. 225) portrays Time as a mythic, transcosmic force weaving a cryptic destiny, its work accompanied by an ominous, funeral chant echoing from the ruins of past civilizations.

Four of the next five poems were originally published in *Revolt*, the short-lived New York anarchist periodical edited by Hippolyte Havel. Benjamin DeCasseres was the magazine's most regular contributor, and *Revolt* offered yet another venue where his work appeared alongside that of radical sculptor Adolf Wolff. The publication also featured letters from Bill Haywood and Margaret Sanger, poems by Nietzsche, and quotations from figures such as Thomas Paine, Max Weber, Octave Mirbeau, Ralph Waldo Emerson, Walt Whitman, and Oscar Wilde—reflecting its eclectic and revolutionary spirit. In contrast to the introspective pessimism and metaphysical despair found in earlier poems, the pieces from *Revolt* are appropriately more political and apocalyptic.

"Across the Gulf" (pg. 233) is a cryptic, oceanic meditation on mortality and metaphysical dread, presenting the sea as both graveyard and unknowable frontier, where human consciousness dares to confront the mysteries of God. "The Conquerors" (pg. 234), published in *Seven Seas Magazine* alongside Franz von Stuck's painting *Der Krieg*, is a vivid poetic indictment of war and the myth of military greatness.

As a personal aside, during the revision process, I typeset a graphical version of "Fifty!" (pg. 237) and posted it on my social media on July 6th, 2025, the event of my own fiftieth birthday, having discovered the poem in the lead-up to my half-century.

More war-themed poems are interrupted by a light poem "On Coney's Beach" (pg. 240) published in the humor magazine *Judge*.

Another departure, "Morning Magic" (pg. 242), evokes the dreamlike exaltation and mythic aspiration found in the fantasy verse of writers like Robert E. Howard and Clark Ashton Smith, blending spiritual yearning with cosmic flight.

The four line "Chatterton" (pg. 243) praises the life and work of Thomas Chatterton, a poet who took his own life at 17, similar to Ben's brother.

In both "Ruins" (pg. 245) and "My Golden Age" (pg. 248), DeCasseres confronts his own life and artistic legacy with a rare degree of directness and mythic self-awareness, something also found in his diaries collected as *Fantasia Impromptu*. "Ruins" presents the poet as a frozen monument to his own inviolable visions—"Vulcan of the exquisite," awaiting decay with stoic grandeur—while "My Golden Age" imagines a posthumous vindication, when the scars of life become transmuted into gold.

Among the non-war poems from 1917, "Similes and a Query" (pg. 257) and "Letter-Boxes" (pg. 258) show DeCasseres working in a more abstract and philosophical mode. In the first, he imagines the human mind as a cosmic force questioning the universe, while in the second, he finds deep meaning in everyday objects, turning letter-boxes into symbols of hope, grief, and unanswered communication.

The one untitled poem (pg. 261) in this volume first appeared in O.O. McIntyre's widely syndicated "New York Letter" column, our example was published in *The Wilmington Dispatch* on February 8, 1918. Introduced as a "startling bit of verse" by "New York's newest poet idol," the poem's appearance in a popular daily three years after the release of *The Shadow-Eater* signals DeCasseres' growing public profile and the recognition of his literary voice beyond small press and bohemian circles. Since this is the only printed example of the poem, I cannot tell if it had a title, or if it is a fragment of a larger work. Oscar Odd McIntyre would feature social updates on DeCasseres regularly in his syndicated column over the next two decades.

The poems from "Birth Mannerisms" (pg. 264) to "Anarch" (pg. 268) are the first batch from a magazine titled *The Quill*, a periodical for the literary set of Greenwich Village, NYC. "Times Schoolhouse" was a sort of poetic essay included in the first edition of *IMP*, but was removed as it departed too much from the poetic form.

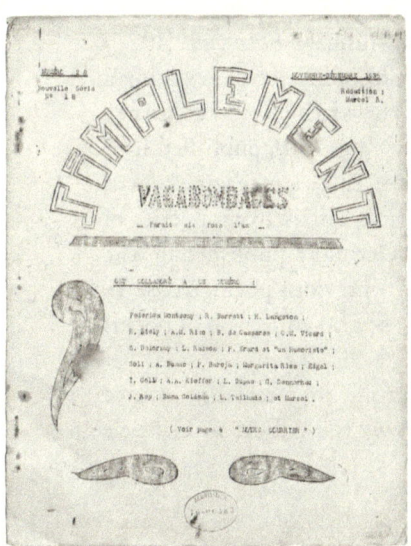

Published in 1918, "The Vampire" (pg. 265) reflects a key moment in the transformation of vampire lore—from folkloric monster to decadent symbol—recasting the figure as a cosmic aesthete who feeds not on blood, but on suns, classical art, and the exhausted spirits of Romantic genius. This poem marks DeCasseres' first notable engagement with the evolving vampire myth in American letters, anticipating his later involvement with *Nosferatu*, where he is credited with writing the English intertitles for the first U.S. release of *Nosferatu the Vampire* in 1929.

Benjamin DeCasseres' 1918 poem "Anarch," (pg. 268) published in *The Quill*, employs a word strikingly uncommon in his time. Clement Wood, in his essay "Jews as Literary Idealists," even captioned a photo of DeCasseres as "The Great Anarch." Unlike *anarchist*, which became the popular form, *anarch* appeared only sporadically in newspapers, sometimes defined as "the author of anarchy" or, quoting *Webster's Unabridged*, "without head or chief." Yet the term carries a deeper literary resonance: Milton in *Paradise Lost* (1667) calls Satan "the Anarch old," Byron in *Childe Harold's Pilgrimage* (1818) condemns "imperial anarchs doubling human woes," and Shelley in *The Triumph of Life* (1822) writes of "the anarch chiefs, whose force and murderous snares / Had founded many a sceptre-bearing line." In the twentieth century James Gibbons Huneker (1857–1921), the American critic of art, music, literature, and theater, revived this Romantic usage by calling composers like Bach and Beethoven "anarchs" of music. DeCasseres, who admired Huneker and published a book of essays about him in 1925, drew from this lineage. Five poems in this volume—"The Cynic of Nazareth" (pg. 90), "Vers Libre" (pg. 179), "A Gray Minute," "An Anarch Minute" (pg. 190), and "Anarch"—use the word directly, portraying the Anarch as a masterless yet masterful figure, a cosmic rebel laughing in defiance of pain. His vision far predates Ernst Jünger's *Eumeswil* (1977), where the "Anarch" emerged as a philosophical type, evoking a philosophical disposition inspired by the writings of Max Stirner.

It is interesting to note that "Italy" (pg. 270), published in *Il Carroccio (The Italian Review)*, August 1918, a magazine geared towards Italians in America, notes that this is from a series of poems dedicated to the opponents of Germany, published in "the August *Chronicle*." It is possible that the previous poem, "Arise Ye Dead!" (pg. 269) is part of that series, but no collection of poems has been located.

Another martial themed poem from an interesting source appears. From a magazine called *Flying* is a tribute to Gabriele

D'Annunzio (pg. 274), a man DeCasseres admired and wrote extensively and frequently about.

Another four poems from *The Quill* in September of 1919 deepen DeCasseres' cosmic vision while applying it to dissonant subjects and stark tonal shifts. Rather than repeating grand metaphysical assertions, he fractures them—"Fantasie" (pg. 279) personifies life's absurdity in a surreal tableau that fuses mathematical abstraction with grotesque myth. "Vicariously" (pg. 280) draws that vision inward, registering spiritual exhaustion not through detachment, but through overwhelmed perception. In "New York" (pg. 281), cosmic rhetoric turns caustic, aimed at the modern city as a machine of death, commerce, and cultural disintegration. It closes the quartet with a godlike self-declaration that is both omnipotent and paradoxically void, reinforcing a recurring DeCasseres motif: the self as microcosm of a universe both sublime and meaningless.

Four poems published between 1920 and 1924 offer a sardonic and celebratory response to Prohibition and its cultural fallout. "Rum's 7 Cardinal Virtues" (pg. 285) mocks the rhetoric of temperance by inverting moral condemnation into a litany of ironic benefits, turning drunkenness into a subversive virtue. "Fermentation" (pg. 286) stretches the metaphor further, portraying intoxication as a vital and universal force animating politics, nature, and art alike. "To the Old Soak" (pg. 290), from 1921, juxtaposes mournful grandeur with comic ecstasy—beginning in the voice of cosmic lament and ending in tipsy revelry thanks to a bootlegged case of Scotch. The second part, with its Whitmanesque catalog of human progress, culminates in a punchline of drunken regression. Finally, "The Bootlegger's Daughter" (pg. 292) turns Prohibition romance into a humorous domestic vignette, full of pet names and moonshine wordplay. Taken together, these poems reflect DeCasseres' at once politically biting and theatrically absurd.

At this stage, near the end of the collection, we are transitioning into mostly previously published work translated into French and published in various papers, mostly associated with the individualist anarchist E. Armand.

Appended to *Chiron the Centaur* in 1937, 15th in the "DeCasseres Book" series, "Codpiece" (pg. 300) offers a mock-heroic finale in the voice of an exalted cosmic egoist. With manic, surreal imagery and comic bravado, it parodies the pose of transcendental self-deification—elevating the speaker above myth, cosmos, and divinity—only to undercut it all with the final punchline: "But I live in a Drain!"

Finis, published by Bio DeCasseres after Benjamin's death in 1945, gathered four late essays that summed up his outlook—meditations on oblivion, the loss of values, and the irrelevance of human striving—written in a plain and final voice. The book closes with his long poem "The Presence: Hymn of a Nihilist to Oblivion," (pg. 303) in which he addresses Oblivion itself as an all-encompassing force: "Being is Thy Space, Will is Thy Time." Here, pride, pain, joy, and even the self dissolve into the silence of the Presence. Both reverent and mocking, the poem turns emptiness into a kind of cosmic hymn. I reprinted *Finis* in full in 2016 together with his diaries (see *Fantasia Impromptu: Finis*, Underworld Amusements, 2016).

Not Included

It's been difficult to determine what should qualify as a "poem" for this collection. I've removed a few pieces that appeared in the first edition and have gone back and forth over many others. Since DeCasseres was never bound by the label of "poet," his epigrams, political *bon mots*, and satirical prose fragments often contain qualities found in poetry—particularly given that he was among the earliest American writers to experiment with free verse. DeCasseres contributed quite a few short pieces to humor magazines such as *Puck* and *The Judge* that are hard

to determine their qualification. "The Coming Slavery," from *Cartoons Magazine*, vol. 17, no. 3 (March 1920), is an example:

> **The Coming Slavery**
> The descent of the Socialist Bomb Squad on the Individualist Club.
> Suppression of the book, "Freedom under the Wage System."
> Soviet investigation of the propaganda for the restoration of free will in private.
> Rigid censorship on papers that cartoon the ruling working classes.
> Exile for those who question the infallibility of the doctrine of Collective Stupidity.

I debated the inclusion of this piece in particular right up until the end, ultimately choosing to present it here in the introduction, preserving it within the project while acknowledging it sits just outside the corpus of what I'm calling "poetry."

Many of these pieces from *Puck* specifically were printed from 1914–1917, where he was listed among the staff of writers alongside James Huneker and George Jean Nathan. It is in *Puck* that I discovered the first known *nom de plume* used by DeCasseres, "Osiris Cobb." Some of his interviews with famous or fictitious people under the assumed name were eventually republished in his book *Forty Immortals* (1926) under his own name.

My final exclusion was the most difficult to make. During the 1930s, DeCasseres shifted his focus to film publications such as *Motion Picture Herald*, but in the last decade of his life he became a regular contributor to the conservative Hearst press. There, he published editorials and book reviews that—especially during the Second World War—grew increasingly patriotic and anti-communist in tone. In the polarized climate of the 1940s, his alignment with American nationalism and his vociferous opposition to communism placed him in a contentious ideological position. On the cultural left, where his name had once appeared alongside anarchists and avant-garde thinkers, he was now dismissed with open scorn. One critic derided him as a man whose "mouth is black with the polish off the shoes of Hearst."

Yet even the far right was not immune from attacking him. In *The Octopus* (1940), a book of anti-Semitic conspiracy theory by Elizabeth Dilling, DeCasseres was listed among Jewish writers supposedly infiltrating the Hearst media empire to defend "Jewish socialism." His patriotic essays were even quoted—ironically—with apparent approval in *Social Justice*, Father Coughlin's notorious publication blending isolationism, anti-communism, and virulent anti-Semitism. That DeCasseres' rhetoric could be embraced in such contradictory circles speaks to both the reach and the ambiguity of his late-career voice.

These final writings were not a betrayal of earlier convictions so much as a theatrical intensification of them. His lifelong Jeffersonian idealism, once cloaked in individualist defiance and Nietzschean aphorism, now appeared dressed in the kitsch and bombast of wartime patriotism. Applauded and denounced from multiple extremes, he remained, to the end, a man unwilling to temper his rhetoric to fit the moment, the difference now is there was an eager and rich publisher for as much of it as could be produced.

Among DeCasseres' voluminous output during this period is a series of highly propagandistic patriotic quasi-poetic pieces— what I've come to call his "Jingo Poems."* Eight of these have been identified from the final years of World War II, appearing in mass-circulation magazines and regional newspapers between 1943 and 1945. Titles like "I Am the United States," "Be an American!" and "If Communism Could Speak" exemplify their tone: populist, fervently nationalistic, and aimed squarely at bolstering the American spirit on the home front. While some retain

---

* The identified titles include: "I Am the United States," *Cosmopolitan* 114, no. 3 (March 1943); "I Am Private Enterprise," *The Milwaukee Sentinel* (Milwaukee, WI), June 27, 1943; "I Am the Treasury of the United States," *The Lexington Advertiser* (Lexington, MS), January 27, 1944; "Spirit of Brotherhood," *Detroit Evening Times* (Detroit, MI), March 19, 1944; "Be an American!," *Detroit Evening Times*, July 15, 1944; "For All Who Labor," *Detroit Evening Times*, September 5, 1944, p. 12; "If Communism Could Speak," *Detroit Evening Times*, July 30, 1945; and "Our Constitution," *Detroit Evening Times*, September 18, 1945.

traces of poetic form, others devolve into unambiguous prose, and all reflect DeCasseres' turn toward kitsch-inflected civic sermonizing. Because of their overtly polemical nature, and their easy availability online through newspaper archives, I have chosen not to include the "Jingo Poems" in this collection.

Among Benjamin DeCasseres' most widely circulated of these pieces is "I Am Private Enterprise," originally published in the *New York Journal-American* and subsequently reprinted across a vast swath of American trade journals, newspapers, and magazines during the 1940s. The piece extols free enterprise in a bombastic, first-person patriotic voice:

> I am the Spirit of Private Enterprise.
> Wherever I have existed freedom of mind and body have existed.
> Wherever I have been murdered by collectivist laws and governmental strangulation freedom of mind and freedom of body have died.
> I was the physical lever of Athenian civilization. I died in the collectivist Feudal ages.
> I was resurrected in the Renaissance, beginning the modern age.
> With the rebirth of free private trading came the vastest expansion in the arts and sciences the world has ever known...

"I am Private Enterprise" became a widely disseminated cultural artifact of wartime and postwar American rhetoric. It was extremely popular with editors of trade magazines, as it was featured in publications with titles such as: *The Builder, Journal of Insurance Information, California Real Estate Magazine, Bulletin of the American Ceramic Society,* and *The National Stationer*. It was even printed in the tens of thousands as a stand-alone pamphlet, ordered by the thousand by civic groups and handed out with other similar tracts. Its reach extended well beyond the business world, being entered into the *Congressional Record* by George B. Schwabe of Oklahoma in 1948. The piece made such a splash that it drew praise from ideological opposites—most notably Ayn Rand, who wrote to DeCasseres in June 1943:

> Thank you very much for your review of my novel *The Fountainhead*. I was glad that you liked Howard Roark. ... I have been a reader of your column for years—in fact, my husband and I take the *Journal-American* because of its columnists. ... If *The Fountainhead* can serve as an introduction, would you let me know and give me an appointment to see you?

Rand's letter underscores not only DeCasseres' cultural prominence during his lifetime but also the lasting impact of his writings on major literary and philosophical figures. Even in the 1940s—decades into his career—his columns still resonated with thinkers like Rand, who recognized in him a kindred spirit and a consistent, defiant voice against collectivism.

•

Following the final poem, I have placed a brief Associated Press portrait of DeCasseres that appeared in *The Arizona Republic* in 1937. It stands not as an epitaph but as an afterimage—a serene coda to the storm of thought and passion that precedes it. In this vignette, the philosopher of negation is shown at ease, ensconced among his books, smiling through the window-light of his later years. I wished the reader, having traversed his abysses, to see him once more in the calm of day—transfigured, almost celestial—as if the restless spirit of his work had found, for a moment, its own quiet heaven.

KEVIN I. SLAUGHTER
*January-November 2013,
revised November 2025*

A Fourth Dimensional Mind
S. P. Rudens

The spiritual forebears of DeCasseres have written his book, the *Forty Immortals*, through him, their living avatar. More than any man breathing in America today, he incarnates the great spirits of all time. In him, as in their works, are made manifest the gestations of their genius—the zenith-reach of their aspirations, the nadir-fall of their tragic failures.

"I partake of the blood and brain and apocalyptic vision of Spinoza," he writes in one of his dynamic revues in this book, and the statement is a literal fact. For through the union of the philosopher's sister Miriam with Samuel de Casseres, he is the blood brother of Spinoza, while any reading of his work will show the spiritual kinship so clearly apprehended and expressed by Don Marquis, when in writing the introduction to his book of verse, *The Shadow-Eater*, he says: "Even when he [DeCasseres, of course] seems to deny God, it is a flareup of the passionate fire of divinity in himself" that really convulses and troubles him.

What Novalis has said of Spinoza has been applied by one of his critics to DeCasseres, too. But, of course, all seekers of a cosmic understanding are God-intoxicated men. All men of genius dwell in the law of this Great Necessity, in this sphere of the Absolute Dimension, where all relativity is merged or, as one may say, indefinitely extended, in an embrace of the Whole. Here the Yea and the Nay are One. Here, as DeCasseres has put it, "All great negations are at last splendid affirmations."

Among moderns, Miguel de Unamuno has well summarized this urge of the human mind to association with the All in its moments of intensest vision when he said:

> I wish to be myself, and without ceasing to be myself to be the others as well, to merge myself into the totality of the cosmos, visible and invisible, to extend myself into the illimitable of space, to prolong myself into the infinity of

---

* *Reflex*, December 1927.

time. Not to be all forever is as if not to be at all. Let me be my whole self for ever and ever. For to be the whole of myself is to be everybody else—to be all or nothing.

The material and spiritual universe can become acceptable to man only when there is nothing external in its infinitude of cosmic associations, when the Whole forms an Absolute in which the All is merged. This is true of the thinking of Unamuno, of DeCasseres, and of all men who face the Great Necessity of cause and significance.

In his *Forty Immortals* DeCasseres bares this merging of great souls in the symbol of Necessity. Even if the roads blazed and trodden by these men be individual and bear unique names, the direction is to a common Ultimate. The lines may be straight or zigzag; the atmosphere may be clear or foggy; the speed be measured by the lightning flash or the wayward will-o'-the-wisp—the end is common even when it seems divergent and in opposition. That is why Spinoza, the outcast of man, reviled by his fellows, seeks reunion with his kind in the incarnation of his Self with the Absolute. That is why Emerson, discontented with the abstraction to which he has reduced the Cosmos, attempts to resurrect it through Self by a union of his Being with the Over-Soul. And even Nietzsche, blasphemer of God and scourger of man, wishes to move on a plane with Deity and so create his dream of Beyond-Man!

DeCasseres shows all these men as improvisers on the grand theme of Destiny—Mystic Trumpeters all, whose paeans of praise or tragic rhapsodies but celebrate the common purpose of life in God. Out of his pages emerges the common theme—the aspects of the Many in the countenance of One. He accepts the prophetic pantheism of Spinoza without rejecting the paganism of Shakespeare. He blasphemes the traitor Fate with Hardy, and with Maeterlinck worships the terror and mystery of the real. He rejects the materiality of possession with Thoreau and embraces the ecstasy and glamor of surrender with D'Annunzio. He knows himself to be part of that cosmic body of which Balzac felt himself, too, an atom, yet, he indulges, at the same time, in the irony of De Gourmont and almost becomes reconciled to the business of playing with him the game of Chance, for the end perhaps of peering into that Wonder which Blake was able to make so luminous and real. In very truth, he is *Chameleon*, though the many moods of his "selves" in this book make him no less keen an instrument of understanding than did his yielding to the moods of his *Forty Immortals* in the book of that name.

Chameleon is a veritable mine of epigram and paradox, a rich quarry of ironic and tragic thought-visions, passions, movements. The expression of it all is personal, intimate, even in its moods of objectivity. His essays on History, on Wonder, on The Irony of Negatives, The Drama of Days, The Passion of Distance, The Artist or The Trail of the Worm, to mention but a few, are so many motivations and affirmations of Self—windows in the edifice of his thought life, lit up by the incandescence of his dynamic vision. His books are spiritual autobiographies. They tell nothing of the movements of his body, for they are the record of his mental "selves" only. As for the latter, they do not always perhaps keep an even pace. They frequently merge and fecundize one another, or clash in internecine war like the ions and elements of the physical universe. They are, like the latter, protean in their transmutations. DeCasseres has a penchant for reading the inductions and deductions of men perversely. By so doing, he annihilates the ordinary bridges of association and by a process of inversion, as it were, transfers the past into the present and future, and makes of Time a whole. This is what he probably means when he characterizes himself as possessing "that marvelous, dangerous gift of seeing everything à rebours—backwards." With this gift, he sees Christ, Buddha and Apollo as so many lights of one common prism, Divinity created by men out of the same matrix of necessity, to serve an identical end. And here Satan is at one with Prometheus, while Ormuzd and Ahriman are but the twin masks of the countenance of one God.

All the work of DeCasseres reveals this mastery of technique, theme and expression. We find it in the *Chameleon*, and in the *Forty Immortals*. We find it also in his *The Shadow-Eater, The Muse of Lies, the Litanies of Negation*, and in the collection of metaphysical tales, dialogues and essays of the imagination he has called *The Eternal Return*.

And when one wonders at the fecundity of the man's mind, at the brilliancy of his epigrammatic *tours de force*, his rhapsodic prose, his prophetic and satiric verse, one is amazed at the failure of his wider recognition. What a miracle of blindness on the part of his contemporaries! Here is a man of indubitable genius, a master of paradox, a transvaluator of values, a worker who transmutes the dark ores of Vulcan into solid objects of strength and of beauty, a Merlin creator of Illusion that seems real—and the cranial walls of Tradition and Babbittry keep him out. Here is a man who has run through the whole gamut of our thinking and whom De Gourmont and Maeterlinck and Thomas Hardy have honored, but whom the Sancho Panzas of our Academies and the Don Quixotes of our Intelligentsia will not pay the homage of a reading.

But as man is constituted, DeCasseres himself perhaps is to blame, save for the fact that the Cosmic Dispenser saw fit to assign to him the task it did, to make him a thinker. To be a thinker is to be one with all, yet to be one—alone. If only the choice spirits of the centuries could all be contemporaries; if man could but live with himself all the time and breed forth sanity from the depths of his own introspection! It were doubtless very desirable to leave these Sancho Panzas and Don Quixotes well alone, then. Unfortunately, one requires a measure of sustenance from the common hoard, while, as one knows, monsters lie in wait in the abysses of one's spiritual loneliness.

DeCasseres knows all this. He knows that the ordinary tale of thee and me suffices for the common man. He knows his bond with him, too. He, also, is "tombed in the belly of Self." He knows it is difficult to eradicate the idols of humanity even in his own brain. His protoplasm, too, quivers with the fever of existence. He differs from his fellows only in that he strives to overcome the infantile virtues of the race, inherent in him, through birth and association; in that he attempts to free himself from the word-fetishisms and the thought-fetishisms that, like barnacles, decay the body of the mind. He views his task as did Ibsen and Dostoyevsky, Nietzsche and De Gourmont before him. He is a dissociator of ideas, a defender of the right of each conception and each word to a freedom of its own—the freedom of evolution and growth—the freedom to become a "sidereal" system, if possible, in the course of its development.

There is more safety in the commonplace. Here every stone is a guide-post to the haven of the sure past. Here one cannot go astray, even when, like Zarathustra in his first Wanderings, one bears the dead burden of a mountebank on his shoulders! To think differently from other men is dangerous. It is to slay Chimera and, like Bellerophon, to scale the sky.

DeCasseres has a symbol for the type of men he represents. He calls himself the Shadow-Eater. He and the men for whom he employs this symbol devour, so to speak, the shadows, the lies that fill the thinking of most of us. That is why Nietzsche dedicates his book to the hierarchy of free spirits of which he deems himself a part and which, he knows, represents but few in number. And so Ibsen when he says, "The minority is always right; the majority is always wrong," becomes literally and truly the "Enemy of the People." And so Dostoyevsky—greatest of all transvaluators of values—makes his Idiot the Christ.

DeCasseres is a Shadow-Eater, the poet, in this other sense, of the intangible, the peruser of realities that the human mind can visualize only as shadows. In it he feels himself "leagued with the Sphinx," or clothed with the night,

> Whose black vapors have filled all the sluiceways of Time—

He feels himself helpless against the night and in his compassion with man and self speaks in defiance of Destiny. His poem "The Vigil" (pg. 98) is a philippic against the Power that shows no pity—that is mute to understanding. In this poem Man beats his head against the rock of futility, while the archfiend Fate returns the shadow-grin of silence as an answer to Man's prayer. "The Vigil" throws a phalanx of hate against the Power that is Destiny. It is, none the less, the lamentation of a soul. Note the tragic irony of its lines:

The Vigil

Here in the naked primal night,
Here where the Veiled sits graven in silence in Its garden
   of weeds,
Here where the Nothing drowses and mutters of a

>   Something to come;
>   Here where the fangs of my soul have fastened at last;
>   Here where through wild-steaming streams of passion
>   and great shroud-like dawns
>   I have dragged my undying Desire—
>   Here, too, will I vigil with Thee through the glutted
>   eternities—
>   Thou imbecile artisan, thou bungler, evader, rhetor and
>   faun!

In his *Litanies of Negation* the symbolism of *The Shadow-Eater* continually recurs. It is the natural formula for DeCasseres' metaphysical nihilism. He is forever "eclipsed" in the "penumbra" of the Infinite, where "nothing changes"; in the "Super-Infinite," also, where "nothing is." "The Specter Life" is truly a shadow. Nothing exists for him and for all:

"Time—the dungeon of Titans,"—annihilates the Whole.

To write a coda on the works of DeCasseres would serve no purpose at this time, or at any time. More so now, when he is still "trapped" in life, when he is "alive" with "the galvanic battery" of his ideas. The ideas of DeCasseres are truly pregnant with electronic power. He who wishes to awaken from his sterility of the moment to the *vita nuova* of his being will find his psychic stimulus in the work of this man.

I have said he is a Nihilist. It is only on the wreckage of the past that we can build. The annihilations effected by the minds of men have always been deeply misunderstood. They do not leave the soil barren at all. On the contrary, the keen ploughs that have furrowed the ground make it ripe for sowing. Annihilations spell re-associations. This is the greatest gift of thought to thought—of man to man. That is the very least with which DeCasseres will reward the reader of his books. We do not need to ask for more.

Benjamin DeCasseres
Blanche Shoemaker Wagstaff

Metaphysics and poetry may seem to be an impossible alliance, especially as the trend of modern verse is in the opposite direction, forswearing symbol and suggestiveness for stark reality. But since the domain of poetics is constantly enlarging, it is not surprising that Benjamin DeCasseres' fearless little volume (*The Shadow-Eater*) is a welcome tribute to individualism and defiance.

Mr. DeCasseres is the super-man fired with Nietzschean verbosity. His chants are bold, sonorous declamations, visioning a nether world, scanning dizzy heights. He leads the reader through a labyrinthine maze, crying: "On! on, my soul thro' the storm, thro' the wrath and terror of death."

He sees life as a pigmy scheme. His gaze is beyond into super-terrestrial realms where man's supreme self-hood stands revealed in all its fullest development. He pictures beings divest of human garb and liberated in infinite spheres. He is the great path-maker, the teacher who "lives behind the mask of things", saying:

> I am the lidless, dispassionate Eye that pierces the murk
>   and the mist.
> I watch and I wait and record—
> I am the shadow that is more real than substance,
> I live and am not, I am the Infinite withered to naught.

Mr. DeCasseres' vision is of a Titan belching forth flame and fury. His phrases are lightening-like invectives that smack of Nietzsche's *Genealogy of Morals*.

His iconoclastic pessimism is malefic, blasphemous. He scorns human life and its futile effort with Promethean contempt. His cynical penetration is the direct offspring of Schopenhauer and Von Hartmann.

> The world is the Temple of Pain grounded and mortised

---

* *The Poetry Journal,* November 1915

> in lies.
> And Love they have sanctified because of its delicate
> tickle...
> I, the eel, that slips thro' the great Bungler's hand, survey
> and judge and cannot be lured by these old temporal
> cozzeners.
> Forever I vanish, I change, yet forever stand firm Flying
> the flag of rebellion.

Many of the poems show that their author knows his Vedanta philosophy by heart. He exults in his detachment from experience:

> Passion, hope, pain, grief, leave me unchanged, (I shed
> universes and moult cycles.)

The following is a clearer note:

> Like a polished pearl hid in a pocket,
> Like lighted tapers set in the murk of a crypt,
> Like the flicker of phosphor on dun seas,
> Like a meteor athwart the heavens of Cimmeria
> So the secret of my soul shines for me in this timeless night.

It is easy to predict that Mr. DeCasseres' poems will remain without adequate comprehension from the public and the casual critic. Few took the trouble to fathom the true purport of *Leaves of Grass*, or *Thus Spake Zarathustra* at the time of their publication. But it is evident there is philosophy in *The Shadow-Eater* that will outlast time itself. The author's almost gruesomely vivid imagery is Poesque, and his lines are pregnant with great truths. His poems are metaphysical meteors, searching, cataclysmic and rich in satire.

The Shadow-Eater is an astounding book of poems. It is a philosophic incantation. Its power is undeniable. Its unpleasant savour penetrates and apalls. There are many ringing lines that scourge and lash and lay bare the piteous heart of man. For Mr. DeCasseres is merciless. Nothing escapes his ruthless inquiry. Life is to him a crystal ball that he shatters with gusty derision. He is the arch-satirist sitting aloft laughing to himself at the caprices and blandishments of humanity. Nothing touches him.

> I am the Spectre at the feasts of the strong men.
> I, neutral, indifferent, sewed up in my silence, my soul the great menstruum of contrasts.

He is the Anti-Christ who salutes :

> Hail, passionate rebel, great anarch of Nazareth, slitter of masks, announcer of self procreate of a self.

The poems most expressive of his clearest vision are "The Sleeper" (pg. 115), "On a Marriage" (pg. 92), and that supreme pæan of penetration, "Love the Destroyer" (pg. 117), beginning:

> I reject Love!
> Love in its sibilant, low-murmured lies, sweet sting of fair bodies, old meat of old Death.

Don Marquis by Eugene Willford "Gene" Markey

Preface (to *The Shadow-Eater*)
Don Marquis

Benjamin DeCasseres strikes us as the most original man writing verse in this country to-day. The more we read his poetry the larger grows our astonishment that he is not more generally recognized and acclaimed for the leader and genius that he is.

He uses the "free verse" form in his compositions; he is the only American poet writing free verse to-day, with the exception of James Oppenheim, who has something unusual and alive and individual to communicate...; he is one of the very few American poets writing any form of verse at any time able to rise up and walk into the cosmopolis where the great intellects of all times dwell and sit down among them with the air of belonging there.

His poetry is the revelation of an intensely religious spirit. Merely that; but that is everything. He is so preoccupied with the thought of God—of all the gods—he sees divine manifestations so clearly in everything that is or has been or may be that he can write of nothing else.

His fervors and revolts and agonies and denials proceed from his attempt to find the relationship of his own soul, of humanity, to the eternal. Even when he seems to deny God it is a flareup of the passionate fire of divinity in himself—the most intensely religious people in all ages have been called atheists by those who did not understand them and who could not see what they saw. They have usually cared little what they were called, being too intent upon peering at the realities behind the veil, which is flesh and rocks and earth, to care.

The effect of the subtlety and strength and insight of DeCasseres is not to be obtained from any one of his poems; you must read all of them.

---

* *The Shadow Eater*, American Library Service (New York) 1923, first printed in his syndicated column.

Don Marquis

I

There was a man in the land of America whose name was Don, and that man was upright and eschewed evil.

Now there was a day when the Sons of Light came to present themselves before the Great Impresario of Spectacles, and Satan came also among them.

And the Great Impresario said unto Satan:

"Hast thou considered Don, that there is none like him, that he is an upright man, one that escheweth evil, one that is beloved of all men and who giveth to his last?"

Satan then answered:

"What wouldst thou with him, Sire?"

And the Great Impresario said unto Satan:

"Strip him of all he hath in the manner of Job".

And Satan then was puzzled, for he knew no sin that Don had committed or why he should thus be in ill-favor with the Great Impresario.

And so he asked:

"But why must this be, Sir? Don is impregnable against all my wiles. Even I, the Supreme Tempter, honor him, knowing that he is sublime in his nature."

Then the Great Impresario, turning his back on Satan, said:

"Do as I bid thee! This man hath in him the unpardonable sin: a sense of humor touching things sacred and divine. Go and do!"

And so that man Don, in the land of America, who was upright and eschewed evil and who was beloved of all men and who gave to his last, had his son taken from him, and then his wife, and then his daughter, and then he was stricken blind, and then he had his second wife taken from him, and then he was paralyzed, and then his speech was taken from him, and then his mind was darkened, and then he was paralyzed again—and thus, utterly helpless and stricken, his properties and moneys were drained from him, and he lay in great agony and weakness until the Great Impresario and his man Satan, seeing that no further evil could be

---

* Published as a pamphlet in 1938 by the author on the occasion of Don Marquis' death.

done unto Don, who was upright, eschewed evil, who was beloved by all men and who gave to his last, sent his soul into the Valley of the Shadow.

II

Again there was a day when the Sons of Light came to present themselves before the Great Impresario of Spectacles, and Satan came also among them, and with him came Don.

And Satan said unto the Great Impresario:

"Behold, Sire, I have brought before thee the man Don who was upright, who eschewed evil and who was beloved of all men and who gave to his last and who has been stripped of all things."

And then Don spake unto the Great Impresario and said:

"Sire, why didst thou do these things to me? I wronged no man in my lifetime and my heart was heavy with love and pity for all who suffered and my hand was ever ready to give.

"But thou, laying on me one great disaster after another as of one who had offended thee overmuch, didst take from me my children, my wives, my sight, my mind, my limbs, my goods and nailed me to a mountain of torture and suffering as was done to Prometheus. Wherefore?"

III

And the Great Impresario of Spectacles of a sudden great gray on his throne, and Satan shriveled up like a man of a thousand thousand years, and the heavens beyond and above and around were slowly flooded as with a silver light.

And rising in the light, filling the heavens to the remotest angles of space, advancing in a gradually closing semicircle over the Great Impresario of Spectacles, came the Angels of Laughter, and they filled the heavens with more numbers than the stars.

And as with one voice the heavens, the stars and the spaces were shaken with the Chant of the Angels of Laughter, and they then shouted:

"Thou, Sire, hath stripped Don, who was upright, who eschewed evil, who was beloved of all men and who gave unto his last, of all but one thing, his sense of Humor, and that clothes him now in triple brass.

"This man is saved, and is even now become one of us, for Laughter is the highest form of Thought and Love.

"Thy kingdoms of Good and Evil, O Great Impresario of Spectacles, are at an end for this earth-freed spirit, for a greater thing hath been found by Don Marquis, the Kingdom of Cosmic Mirth, the Laughter that topples gods from their thrones, and against that nought shall prevail!"

And Don the well-beloved, Don the sublime, Don the Poet, Don the Wit, Don who was stripped of all things in the manner of Job was lifted high into the Light by the healing Angels of Laughter, and his soul was carried into the Valhalla of Triumphant Mirth, where he shall reign as a shining spiritual presence while there still lives on Earth a single man or woman who knew DON MARQUIS.

Foreword (to *Anathema!*)
Eugene O'Neill

For too many years Benjamin DeCasseres has spilled his glittering fancies on a deaf American ear. He has had the fabulous adventures of a philosopher who could not abandon nor deny his poetic gift. He could not turn professional and expound a system in the thick verbiage which might awe his colleagues. Nor could he descend to the level of a daily message in juicy platitudes for the tabloid mind. In such a plight, he has had little welcome in the academy and none in the crowd. All his soaring has been lonely.

To be a true philosopher in America is almost to invite oblivion. It is only fake philosophers who thrive here. Their formula is thoroughly standardized, and only requires a persistent, brainless application. One need only have a message plain or vague enough to mean nothing and announce it with a solemn countenance and an oracular bray.

DeCasseres has always been on the loose, chasing the tail of the ultimate word. It does not matter particularly to him whether he belongs as philosopher or poet or mystic. His is a capricious mind and a vagrant one. He can be goatish or severe, ricocheting or pyrotechnical. He insists in and out of season upon recording the ascending line on the graph of his soul.

An inebriate of sonorities, he chants disillusion and raises his panegyrics to the sky. He is swift, orgiastic and inexhaustible. He cries out his negations with a huge and resonant *YES!* He is that phenomenal ironist who does not want to be gentle, who must be supremely contemptuous and fiercely assertive.

There is nothing native about DeCasseres in the sense that he picks up the philosophical mantle where it was dropped by his immediate predecessors. The whole Concord School and the pragmatists could have spared themselves a single furrow on the brow so far as any influence on him is concerned. Nor have any of the laborious inductive thinkers left a scar upon his mind. Hair-splitting has never been in his line. He never troubles with the question of the essential validity of ideas as such. Nor does he argue the fine points of thinking as a theory. Neither classification of causes nor explanations of them on the basis of accumulated data gleaned from the observation of the workings of so-called natural laws appear anywhere in his writings. By such definitions he is no philosopher at all.

His sources must be sought elsewhere. The scientists and metaphysicians would be quick to disown him. The mystics and poets might claim him as one of their own, but would look suspiciously upon his passion for doubt and his relentless questioning. Among them he would be a heretic too. If such genealogy counts for anything, he can be traced, among the philosophers, to Schopenhauer and Nietzsche, a hybrid product mixing despair and rhapsody.

Among the poets, he stems from the ecstatic writers of the Psalms, and infiltrates his blood with the rough-house of the tavern. He can stand with one foot on a brass rail, raise his glass high in the air and intone a chorus, part Dionysian, part biblical, and the rest elegiac.

DeCasseres has undertaken the herculean job of carving his own niche as a writer in America. It is hardly likely that he will ever achieve wide public acceptance. Nor does it appear that he will be made the object of careful critical scrutiny by some small group of pedants who might get a thesis out of him as an American phenomenon.

He is too abstract for the one and too extravagant for the other. Ignored by both, his work gets only occasional publication. In truth, he is crushed between the upper and nether millstones. He is looked upon, when he is discussed at all, as a freak who is exploding with metaphors and a dazzling, colossal vocabulary. To the general reading public he is practically unknown. The schools have probably never heard his name, and would give it very scant consideration if it were forced upon them.

With whom or with what system, then, can his name be linked? What studies has he made of space and time and transcendental reasoning? To what established category can he be assigned and by what respected right has he come to the title of philosopher? None whatever. By any such reckoning, he is an outsider. He will have to get along under the designation of an unphilosophical philosopher.

When DeCasseres is mentioned in the prevailing literary chat, it is usually as the chronicler of an almost forgotten, bibulous New York. He is thought of as a post-mortem bard of the pre-Volsteadian era. In the minds of those who have only read his odes to Gambrinus, he stands for a quaint old bibber who is now reminiscing regretfully on the good old days.

Anathema! should dispel such fantastically idiotic notions. The essence of DeCasseres' driving imagination is to be found in these *Litanies of Negation*. To me *Anathema!* is a unique and inspiring poem. It plagues and provokes the mind. Its vigorous figures and its exalted invective give it immense power. Racing upward, it heaps crescendo upon crescendo. It is chaotic, extravagant, brilliant, derisive with a Satanic grin and drenched with rich imagery.

Anathema! is far more than a hymn of renunciation. It is the torment and ecstasy of a mystic's questioning of life. The answer comes alternately as *yes* and *no*. And because the emphasis has been placed on the *no*, DeCasseres has convinced himself that he has said the final negative. It is not so. He is the "scorner of Gods and humans" and promises "salvation in a sneer." He carouses in his "inextinguishable laughter" and goes dizzy-sick on a "vintage headier than Hope." Trying to shout down the clamor in his brain with a crashing *NO*, his ecstasy overpowers him and sings its own affirmation. Benjamin DeCasseres is the poet who affirms the chaos in the soul of man. His *no* is a *yes!!*

Robinson Jeffers: Tragic Terror

It is as difficult to conceive Robinson Jeffers in any other place than Carmel, California, as it would be to think of Shelley living in Whitechapel, Dostoyevsky at Narragansett Pier or William Blake in Pittsburg. If ever a man and the Spirit of Place had conspired for a mystical union it is here.

That portion of California—its hills, sea, blue lupins, golden poppies, sea-gulls, dirt roads, pines, firs, hawks, herons and light-houses—stretching between Point Joe and Point Lobos (roughly, about thirty miles) belongs as absolutely to Robinson Jeffers, poet of Tragic Terror, as Wessex belongs to Thomas Hardy. This place has chosen this man to tell its secret spiritual and physical tragedies to the world and to voice its bitter beauties in his long-rolling, crashing, choppy lines: the transfiguration in his sensibility of the brawling harmonies and bickering winds of the sea. His work is the colossal symphony of a mad Dante.

Jeffers—stark, elemental, monk-like—has grown into the landscape. He is physically part of the fauna and flora. He has coupled with this sky, this earth and this sea on the iron beds of his consciousness. Unearthly, twisted, gnarled, weird, diabolically beautiful Point Lobos has whispered into his ear, as a tree once whispered into the ear of another, "Thou untold life of me!"

The wind and the sea have wrought the trees at Point Lobos and the adjacent hills to grotesque and macabre shapes. By day unearthly, by night it is ghostly. From it stream the elemental and demoniacal psychical forces that engulf the whole coast to Monterey. It needs the genius of Poe, of Lafcadio Hearn, of Chopin, of Dore, of Baudelaire, of Jeffers to translate into art-forms the overwhelming emotion of brutal beauty and abysmal melancholy that Point Lobos inflicts upon the sensitive, receptive soul. Here damnation and the forbidden well out of the very rocks. In all the world no fitter place could have been found to conceive and give birth to

---

* Benjamin DeCasseres, "Robinson Jeffers: Tragic Terror," *The Bookman* (New York) 66, no. 3 (November 1927); reprinted as a pamphlet (privately printed by John S. Mayfield, 1928) and later collected in *The Elect and the Damned* (Blackstone Publishers, 1936)..

the tremendous tragedies of Robinson Jeffers. His steel-muscled genius has lifted Carmel to Golgotha.

When I read Jeffers' "Tamar" and "The Coast-Range Christ" I get a feeling of vastness that I have experienced only in Aeschylus, Shakespeare, Hardy and Whitman. There is for me no vastness, for instance, in the pages of Balzac or Dostoyevsky. Depth, height—yes. Vastness—no. Vastness is a quality that is psychically communicable. In Jeffers' work—even in his smallest poems—this vastness is implicit. It is the sense of the eternal and the fatalistic not, as a passing mood, injected or worked into the poem for the purpose of artistic effect, but as something in which Jeffers, like Hardy and Whitman, perpetually lives, moves and has his being.

Vastitude may be an inherent quality in the minutest bit of creative work, in the smallest figure by Rodin, two simple lines of Blake, three words of Jeffers, and may be totally absent in great masses—Dreiser's work or the work of H. G. Wells, for instance. Take this from "Tamar":

> O beauty of the fountains of the sun,
> I pray you enter a little chamber,
> I have given you bodies, I have made you puppets,
> I have made idols for God to enter
> And tiny cells to hold your honey.
> I have given you a dotard and an idiot,
> An old woman puffed with vanity, youth but botched
>   with incest,
> O blower of music through the crooked bugles,
> You that make signs of sins and choose the lame for angels,
> Enter and possess. Being light you have chosen the dark
>   lamps,
> A hawk the sluggish bodies; therefore God you choose
>   Me; and therefore I have made you idols like these
>   idols to enter and possess.

The cold tragic beauty of "Tamar", "Roan Stallion", "The Tower Beyond Tragedy", "The Coast-Range Christ" and "The Women at Point Sur" is also a perfect reflection of the man, who is cold.

He burns with a white fire. He tells his story in these poems with the sublime aloofness of a being who has dismissed life as an ethical problem entirely from his consciousness—if it was ever there. Life is a play of forces, of which the dramatic values alone concern him. He records it with a brutal negligence. Those magnificent and beautiful Choroses and Antichoroses in "The Coast-Range Christ" are cold, incandescent suns that revolve above the tragedy of the boy slacker. They are as inhuman, as impersonal, as melodiously sublime as the God of Spinoza and Hardy—the Hardy of "The Dynasts".

This is from "The Coast-Range Christ":

> When God was made man he had something to suffer, a
> story of a stable, and to weep and be wounded,
> Little clods on great glory, and suddenly he soared Wide
> of the Syrians and Romans, and the world that they
> ravaged was an atom in a multitude, surrounded
> By the splendor of the dawn's lamps dancing to their Lord.

Jeffers' mysticism is the mysticism of pantheism. All is in God, God is in all things. Everything exists in the glamor of Spirit—his clouds, his herons, his sea-fogs, his characters, even Woodrow Wilson. Whatever is is poetic, mysterious, frail effigies of reality, blown bubbles of ecstatic and satanic gods. Tremendously real, vital and wide-awake in his visualized descriptions, Jeffers contrives by the magical powers of his genius to make an object or a character both familiar and unfamiliar to us under the same light. Each thing is seen simultaneously under the aspect of time and eternity—a house, a tree, a nymphomaniac, an idiot, a sheriff, a sea-gull, a crazy messiah.

This is to the "matter-of-facts" boulder with which he built his forty-foot Hawk Tower:

> To The House I am heaping the bones of the old mother
> To build us a hold against the host of the air;
> Granite the blood-heat of her youth
> Held molten in hot darkness against the heart Hardened

> to temper under the feet
> Of the ocean cavalry that are maned with snow
> And march from the remotest west.
> This is the primitive rock, here in the wet
> Quarry under the shadow of waves
> Whose hollows mouthed the dawn; little house each
>   stone
> Baptized from that abysmal font
> The sea and the secret earth gave bonds to affirm you.

Behind every page of Jeffers stalks Fatality, tall as the stars and as serenely implacable in its trajectories and orbits. With "unhurrying feet" it overtaxes its predestined victims. It moves like a murkey-luminous cloud over the five tragedies of Jeffers—world-old gigantic cloud that conceals the thunderbolt forged in the bone and blood and flesh of the ancestors of all the characters. Fatality is of the essence of tragic beauty, and nowhere have I found it more completely and clearly expressed than in "Tamar". There is only one tragedy in the whole world's literature that I would rank with "Tamar" from the angle of fatality, and that is the *Oedipus Rex* of Sophocles.

> Who has ever guessed to what odd ports, what sea
>   buoying the keels, a passion blows its bulkless
> Navies of vision?
> * * * * * * * you'll learn when you have lived at the
>   muddy root
> Under the rock of things; all times are now, today plays
>   on last year and the inch of our future
> Made the first morning of the world.

Those long-rolling lines of Jeffers have for me the lyrical grandeur of epochs of time, of the tides of circumstance In his mastery of this form he is superior to either Whitman or Blake. They unfurl on the page out of the soul of Jeffers himself. They are a continuation of the sea in his brain. They lap and curl and crash in mile-long heaves. Rough-hewn like the massed battalions of storm clouds on the horizon of his Pacific, they advance on the reader interlapped, uneven, crenellated, and fall with a crash on the ear. They flood the sockets of the aesthetic senses with a curious music:

> The year went up to its annual mountain of death,
> gilded with hateful sunlight, waiting rain.
> Stagnant waters decayed, the trickling springs that
> all the mistyhooded summer had fed
> Pendulous green under the granite ocean-cliffs dried
> and turned foul, the rock-flowers faded,
> And Tamar felt in her blood the filth and fever of
> the season.

There is nothing extraneous in Jeffers' work. It is dense, compact, a pattern woven by a man who takes every stitch with precision and who has plotted out the whole scheme and is complete master of it. There is not a superfluous line in all his poetry. It is an arterial, a ganglionic system, to remove one tiny bit of which would cause the story of the poem to bleed to death.

I know of no two more perfect works of art, as art, in the whole range of dramatic literature than "Tamar" and "The Coast-Range Christ". They are, structurally, vast and perfect cathedrals of words. His sunrises, his sunsets, his creeks and his herons, what appear superficially as his lyrical asides and divagations, are part and parcel of the unfolding drama. It is a blending of spiritual and material scenery. The dramas in the hearts of his men and women are meshed with the elements, with the slow-revolving panorama of the California year. All that is his *mise-en-scène* for the catastrophic lives of men and women on a tiny star moving *con furia* from nowhere to nowhere in the mathematical pandemonium of the spheres.

His "obscurity"—and he is "obscure" at times—is the obscurity of an unexpected individualization of language, a sudden eruption into our anemic, sleek and dutiful prose and poetry of a powerful and original genius whose expressional roots are in himself. When I have come across passages in his volume that seem obscure, I put it down to my own obtuseness. I should clamber up to his thought. There is no reason why he should descend to me. I have paused many times to get at the heart of words, startling flights into the star-jungles of far etymological heavens, and I have always been rewarded by dragging up from my thought and Jeffers' "obscurity" amazing and dazzlingly beautiful treasures. And yet how simple he can be, too!—

"The sweet and female sea."
"The sea moved on the obscure bed of her eternity."
"The maggot's music in the tube of a dead ear."
"We must keep sin pure or it will poison us."
"The lusts of his youth lead him to paw strange beds."
"She has also a monkey in her mind."
"I am the bloodstain on the doorsill of a crime."

Besides "The Women at Point Sur" incest is the theme of "Tamar" and "The Tower Beyond Tragedy", while "Roan Stallion" tells of the love of a woman for a horse. Which recalls to me an incident that occurred when I was visiting Jeffers at Carmel.

Jeffers and I were talking of the literature of incest when Mrs. Jeffers said:

"Robin, when will you quit forbidden themes?" (Jeffers had just then finished "Roan Stallion".)

For answer, Robin smiled—a smile enigmatic and unanswerable, a smile that came nearer to the smile of Mona Lisa than any I have ever seen on the human face. It seemed to say to me, "I shall change my themes when the heart of man and woman changeth—which will not be tomorrow!"

Incest as a theme has been used by Aeschylus, Sophocles, John Ford, Shelley and Wagner. One recalls also *Hamlet* and the Dane's denunciation of his mother "posting to incestuous sheets". It is the least explored of all "complexes" and is the most fertile in dramatic and tragic possibilities. It can only rise above the level of the pornographic and "forbidden" (what is forbidden in nature?) in the hands of a great tragic writer like Jeffers and his literary ancestors. You must see from the heights of the gods to portray what goes on in hell.

"The Coast-Range Christ" is a tremendous piece of irony—the fate of a lad in the Carmel hills who slacked on war-registration day in the name of Christ. It is vivid and breath-catching. David Carrow is a religious neurotic and a Joseph before his seductress, and across the pages of this tragedy there lies the sneer of the gods at the comedy of Christianity.

Never in all the history of prose and poetry has there been attempted such a satanic transvaluation of all earthly values as in "The Women at Point Sur". The Rev. Dr. Barclay, who moves through this longest of Jeffers' tragic poems, after fifteen years of chastity proclaims himself God on the hills of Carmel. He is God turned Anti-Christ. He is Zarathustra-Satan, an illuminated incarnation of the New Evil, a post-war immoralist and dethroner of reason magnified to cosmic proportions. Mephistopheles, Iago and Vautrin are Boy Scouts compared to this tremendous being who an nounces that "all is permitted"—rape, incest, murder and war—in the making of the New Race.

> He will have confusion for its beauty, he is wild to walk in
> new ways, he snatches at the rose burning,
> He stirs in the earth * * * * *
> The God of the stars has taken his hand out of the laws
> and has dropped them empty
> As you draw your hand out of a glove.

He possesses his own daughter, April, to test his faith in his own Godhead, for "God is action", and he, the Rev. Dr. Barclay, is God.

He gathers disciples, lesbians, clairvoyants, drunkards, lust-swollen farm hands—all is permitted them; there is no longer any "good" or any "evil" in the world. The old idols are smashed.

> "I tell you I have seen in the fountains of God destruction
> standing
> With stone hooves on the cities. * * * *
> Doing has no thread to thinking, nobody knows
> What's made in the dark water till it pops the surface."

Jeffers, in this poem, like Nietzsche in *Thus Spake Zarathustra*, seems to be a precursor of the Great Terror that the human race approaches, of which the war gave us but a momentary flash. In the "vast insanity of things" only Power shall be God.

This poem of one hundred and seventy-one close-knitted and swiftly-revolving pages of drama, tragedy and abnormal frenzies is illuminated with that magic of metaphor and simile that puts Jeffers toweringly above his age. The light that falls from this book is from the crackle and flames of warring black suns, sinister, haunted, ghastly.

There is a superb hidden sensuality in Jeffers, pagan and Dionysiac. His poem "Fauna" is one of the finest things in the language, Swinburnian in its lyrical love-passages:

> Would God the sun that kissed your body brown
> Had been my mouth, Fauna, or mine the white
> Teeth of bold waves that bite
> Your heedless ankles when you wander down
> To dance under the dunes a moonlit night.

And what is the philosophy, the metaphysic, the religion of Robinson Jeffers? It is here, I believe, in "Roan Stallion":

> Humanity is the start of the race; I say
> Humanity is the mold to break away from, the crust to
>   break through, the coal to break into fire,
> The atom to be split.
> Tragedy that breaks man's face and a white fire flies out of
>   it; vision that fools him
> Out of his limits, desire that fools him out of his limits,
>   unnatural crime, inhuman science,
> Slit eyes in the mask; wild loves that leap over the walls of
>   nature, the wild fence-vaulter science,
> Useless intelligence of far stars, dim knowledge of the
>   spinning demons that make an atom,
> These break, these pierce, these deify, praising their
>   God shrilly with fierce voices.

It is the philosophy of the superman. It is the mystical dream of Nietzsche.

Robinson Jeffers is barely forty. He is the greatest event in American literature since Whitman. He is a Colossus, and already is an immortal—at least among those who instinctively feel the difference between the men of the hour and the men of the century.

In his work there is a wild, dishevelled, remote beauty and the music of an infernal but contained madness.

The Shadow-Eater
(1915, 1917, 1923)

The Protagonist

To Carlo de Fornaro

Medusa! I go toward you smiling, serene; my will is granite to your stare, and I have that within me which blows out the light of hells set there within your eyes and turns to mottled stone the serpents on your head.

I have woven of my pains a masque of bronze and the summits of my deepest hells are changed into the impetuous lightnings of my will and claws of steel have come to grow upon my mutilated members.

I have violated my own graves and set the skeletons of my selves at my meal-less feasting board, and still found tender meat upon their bones, and the marrow of their ancient griefs was as hippocrene to me.

Eternity! Infinity! I come toward thee swifter than a thought of death! I come toward thee bulging like a woman in her ninth month!—bulging with my hells, my devils, my Gethsemanes, booty of my sullen pride!

Tantara! Tantaro!

Death-lights on the scud and the baying of wind in the rigging, the hail on my cheek—
                Tantara! Tantaro!
The wheel in my hand is shattered by a bolt from On High, chart and compass are lost in the coiling dun sea—
                Tantara! Tantaro!
Scuttle me? Yea, scuttle me—I'll bob up again, not in smooth waters but there where the storm is the wildest—
                Tantara! Tantaro!
Didst Thou think to awe me, me the unhallowed, the daring, the storm-cleaver, the seeker in gutter and star?—
                Tantara! Tantaro!
I am lashed to myself, to the iron mast of Necessity, and Thy scourgings I use for my rivets—
                Tantara! Tantaro!
Ballast and cargo and anchor, all have been jettisoned into Thy seas—
                Tantara! Tantaro!
On! On! my soul through the storm, through the wrath and the terror of death—
                Tantara! Tantaro!

The Tongueless One

There stands that Mute into whose ear the ages have whispered
　　their secrets—
There stands that Mute with lusting eye and lusting ear who
　　uttereth naught—
Mute of a myriad secrets who knoweth whither we wend;
Mute of the graven face and the alabaster hands—
There before me stands that Mute whose earthly name is Death—
That Mute into whose monstrous ear all things are whispered but
Who *uttereth naught.*

The Shrine in the Mist

I travel toward a Shrine that is set in a mist—long have I been on
    the way.
I hear dull rasping whispers afloat on the night:
Are they spirits conferring, friendly to me and my journey,
Or the half-smothered mockeries of the fiends that I know?—
They that sneer and pass on the winds in the night.

I travel toward a Shrine that is set in a mist—
By day I am beset by the beasts of my nethers and awed by the old
    bleached cadavers that strew the intricate alleys of vision.

I peer at you, O glutton, well-fed, nigger-hipped, bag-eyed; at you
    I am peering,
And wonder whether the Shrine is hid in the mists of your guts—
Wondering whether the Truth be not a belch and a glass and a
    lusty young wench.
And I peer at you, too, O Gautama, the purpled renunciant, great
    Shadow-Eater:
I peer at you there on the roadside, where you sit 'neath the Bo
    tree,
Motionless, graven as death, solved in thy pulseless Nirvana—
Wondering whether the Shrine is hid in the mists of thy brain.
Am I mocked? Am I followed? Who goes there? Hands off! thou
    Vile Thing!
Thou knowest not me nor the thing that I seek:
The Shrine that is set in a mist—over There, just Beyond.

My Comic Perspective

When a boy I was wrenched in a gin hidden in a garden of roses:
    thus am I lame.
Later was slugged on the head by the Father of Lies—the Ideal:
But I laughed and hallooed, "Come, To-morrow!"

I have been bushwhacked by women, gnawed to the bone by a
    great ancient lust:
All things I touched turned slime-green
And black—hideous thoughts played 'round my night-pillow like
    rats 'round the new-dead:
But I laughed and hallooed, "Come, To-morrow!"
I used to say, "God?—why, that is myself!"
The world took me seriously, set me up for a savior: But I laughed,
    doffed aureole, and hallooed, "Come, To-morrow!"

Then I donned horns and tail and cried, "Behold! I am Lucifer!"
So they stoned me till I looked like a shambles:
But I laughed and hallooed, "Come, To-morrow!"

I bought from a drab a filthy old handkerchief, exhibited it as the
    Veil of Isis.
The popes of philosophy bowed down to me and mumbled
    "Eureka!"
But I laughed (for I knew) and hallooed, "Come, To-morrow!"

Well, here am I now, a butt-end, awaiting translation.
The world I have found a small box with endless false bottoms;
I have come to the tomb, a little clay box which, too, is false
    bottomed:
I call into it, laugh and halloo, "Come, To-morrow!"

The Peeper

I am an eavesdropper, a peeper, a cosmic footpad;
With my ear at the keyhole of Eternity I report what I hear in that beyond-room, where It works—
It, the thwarter of me and of thee and of all things that savor of smut and of ether—
Thwarts even itself in its huge imbecility: It, the spirit of Law, the shadow of thee and of me,
The Great Blunted Purpose.
What I hear in the beyond-room, is it the illusions of dreams, the crackle of burning brain-faggots,
Or the veritable It at its experiments?—
Solving us, evoking us, tempting us out of the womb of the Naught into the awareness called life.
Does It use the dregs of me or the best of me?
Eternity: is it inhabited?
The imminent cycles, the durations dead, the secrets in them: are they in Its keeping?
Still, I listen, with my eye at the keyhole, and report;
For I know there are a Thwarter and one thwarted, a Nothing at war with a Something,
A gad and a writhe—
One who returns everlastingly, but who is never repeated in Time.

The-Circle-That-Looks-Like-A-Line

I am the Watcher, and me nothing eludes.
I live behind the mask of things,
My breath is world-wither, and a chance shot from my eye-
    sockets confounds the God of Illusions at Its imbecile
    pastimes.
I stand within Time's crumbling walls and weave at Eternity's
    looms
The Circle-that-looks-like-a line.
I am leagued with the Sphinx, and her secretive mumblings I
    alone understand.
I am the footnote that explains that old undecipherable
    palimpsest called Life,
And it is for me the drum beats—the deadly intoning drumbeats
    that the mummer Man jigs to.

Briskly Man in his morn steps forth, guards up.
He bows, he smiles, and his eyes, foci of his myriad lusts,
Seek in the dust for the thing that slipped, eel-like, through his
    fingers in the yesterdays.
At night, within his locked and barred room, his hope-fattened
    face dismantles.
His eyes grow knotted lights, jaws sag—weary, oh, weary is he!
Pain! Pain! gay-pain! I watch, I record, in
The Circle-that-looks-like-a-line.

Youth! Youth! how gay his step!
His soul scents Truth—he is off like a hound on the trail, white
    brow upturned, the old ecstatic urge in his eye:
His hands would hook her now!
Up! Up! he reaches and steps off the precipice of the world.
A Hag bends over him, a Hag whose face is a lutescent leer,
Eyes steel-grayed by a knowledge of the pitiless truths.
Eternity rings with her glee-shrieks as she gathers his bones—
Bones that shall feed her quenchless immemorial fires in the
    nether hollows—
Hollows of the mocking shapes,

Hollows of metallic laughs,
Hollows of the wan gray spectres.
Pain! Pain! gay-pain! I watch, I record, in
The Circle-that-looks-like-a-line!

Yea, I am the lidless, dispassionate Eye that pierces the murk and
    the mist—
My tears are a laughing,
My laughing a weeping—
I watch and I wait and record,
Brooding over my soul, that dried lava-stream and granary of
    volcanic dust;
Brooding over my brain, that mirror of the implacable trivial.

I am a shadow that is more real than a substance,
Am skewered and pinioned to offal—yet my soul is a
Kremlin of unapprehended magnificence,
The Vision Malefic and the Vision Beatific, too.
I live and am not, am the Infinite withered to naught.

I watch, I record, and I weave at Eternity's looms
The Circle-that-looks-like-a-line.

My Divine Hate

Ever-changing, ever-vanishing, an evocation from out the Mist,
Tottering forever to a doom that is never pronounced,
I am the visible Invisible,
The eel that slips through God's hands,
A dominoed Abstraction whose lineaments the most curious
    cannot discover,
Renascent over your head when you think I lie dead,
Intruder in Time, enclayed for a moment, flinty, brittle,
Flying the flag of Rebellion, chanting my hates and my dreams.

The world is the Temple of Pain grounded and mortised in lies—
And that which they have told you is good I say is maggoty with
    lies.
Hope is a whore and love is a lie and a flea has more for his labor
    than a man,
The wisest of whom is still earth's awkward buffoon.
To-morrow is God—they have added a jot to Eternity!
Know they not to-day is Eternity and to-morrow its lewd,
    beckoning shadow?
And love they have sanctified because of its delicate tickle.
Pah! this rotten old breeding-patch circling the sun!

From the center to circumference, from nadir to zenith,
I, the eel that slips through the Great Bungler's hands, survey
    and judge
And cannot be lured by these old temporal cozzeners.

Yea, forever I vanish, I change, yet forever stand firm,
Flying the flag of Rebellion from the Temple of Pain,
Knowing the Thing that skulks in the adytum.

The Rotted Ideal

Framed in ebon memories her picture hangs there upon the walls of my brain.
'Tis not the face I put there in my youth: that glorious youth of me,
Slain by its lusts, bitten to death by the baby vampires that swarmed in its blood.
The lost woman of my soul! warm lips, black eyes—
Face that was a prism of love shot through by the rays from some dumb despair—
Long has it vanished.
And the dust of my acts have gathered on that brow,
And my sins have smitten her cheeks to a pallor, and her eyes welter in two brackish tears—
Tears that have lain stagnant in those bony cups for a myriad soul-cycles.

I have wrought my own decay into that face: it has traveled the way of my own dissolution.
Will it break on my brain-walls and streak all my rottenness anew?
And a spider has woven a web over and around the great frame of ebon
And the thin bladder of flesh that once was her face—A leering, grinning spider has woven his web there,
A leering, grinning spider whose mouth sucks poison from her lips.
Lead on, hell-lights!

The Vision Malefic

My soul is a tarn as black and motionless as the night above
In which whirl forever and ever the pallid balls of light that are
    my sickly dreams.
I am weaving a shroud for the God whom I hate—I have defied
    him and cursed Him, and here is His winding-sheet.
I am lodged in my sins, and my soul is lean of its lusts.
The worm that gnaws at the breast of the maid new dead—that is I,
And the bell that tolled her to rest—I am that toll.
My heart ventricles are like the bases of canyons untouched by
    the sun.
I am dried, bleached and blanched, lie stark in a great pestilent
    vapor,
And Time feeds at my brain like the vultures at the heart of
    Prometheus:
Who will shrive me and draw the lids over these eyes?

Dying

There he lies, his pale face fitfully waving a truce to Old Care,
Life flowing out from a million invisible rents in his soul,
To-morrow finally abolished.
To-night he still breathes,
To-morrow he'll lie with the breathless,
Past the goal, uprendered, solved in black mist, domino doffed—
    no more.

O Life, thou plunderer,
Sly in thy cozzening, fell in thy lusts, weaver of nightmares, liar
    and cheat,
Here is thy last mockery,
Here is thy quarry: hast signalled the worms even now?
Swift be thy flight, thou craven and satyr and old purpled lust!

The Dead Who Live

Up from the nether world in unending procession,
Like the lurid mists at the dawn-time,
Like the black wraiths that ascend from foul crypts,
Arise and ever arise my impulses.
Across the field of consciousness they stalk,
An-hungered, lust-ravened, lean of their ghastly dreams—
Thou devils of the gone-by!

Exvolved

I am the Spectre at the feasts of the strong men and sneer at their
    brag.
I listen where the weak wail and sneer at them, too, for their wail
    is old Envy masked as Humility
The strong shall be tricked out of their strength, I say,
And knock at the doors of the weak for a dole of black bread;
The weak shall become strong, I say, and burrow their way into
    the thrones of the mighty.
The pieces are changed, the game is eternally the same.

Only I shall persist in an eternal likeness unto myself—
    I, neutral, indifferent, sewed up in my silence, my soul the
    great menstruum of contrasts,
The Heel and the Worm.

The God of Negation

I have ascended to the topmost spaces and dragged the cars of the
    devildare gods from their courses;
They saw me not, but felt me as a Presence that hurled them from
    the track.
I have in a wondrous Thought undermined the Milky Way
    and have sown the orbits of the suns with dragons' teeth
    uprooted from my rebellious soul:
Those eyes of gleaming fire saw me not, but felt me as a movement
    in the Abyss.
I have numbed the arm of the blind old Artisan, and he shall die
    at my last Epiphany:
He heard me not, but felt me as the great Destructive Presence.

Godward

God?—the sum of my tendencies, uttered, unuttered, definite, innate;
Me the individual, my special differentia—not thee, but me unevolved, guessing at myself unegged;
That is God if God there be.
Christ was the deepest, Napoleon was the deepest, he of Weimar was the deepest:
To be yourself, that is the deepest—
That is to be God.

Thou shalt love thyself more than thy neighbor.
Sound trumpet, thrust rapier, cleave unto thyself: self-ward we go, godhood be ours!

Unique in all time is my unquotable self:
God in the dungeon of me, fear-shackled, thonged in the cords of the past.
Into the light at this moment, thou long-buried One;
Sternly, defiantly, joyously, I lift Thee into the light!
Long hast thou lain in crypts, and thy eyes are still closed;
Mute is God's tongue, as silent as dreams.

Sound trumpet, thrust rapier, I cleave to myself, though spiked to a cross and rabbled by Doubt!

Beyond Sense

My brain is the haunt of a naked Curiosity that has lured my soul
 across the purple bars of sense,
Beyond the last outpost of Reason, where I know not if I be I.
Lights quicken and wane, glooms thicken around me and break
 into lean and hurrying Shapes—
Supraterrestrial phantoms, spectral norms of this world and
 vague patterns of things not yet become.
Forest of branching selves, my various masks, my serio-comic
 souls,
My antique, half-remembered egos: are ye that?
And here I now stand peering tensely curious into the crater of
 Eternity,
Seeking out Demiurge there in the depths,
When the truth flashes on me: I am but fume, spew, from that
 Depth—
I and thee, all, but fantastic smoke-shapes flitting above the crater
 of Eternity;
And Demiurge, muttering, retreating, advancing there in the
 Depths, is but the shadow of
Me the Curious One.

The Cynic of Nazareth

The keenest Cynic of them all: Jesus Christ!

Hail! passionate rebel, great anarch of Nazareth, slitter of masks,
Announcer of Self procreate from a self—
Halloo! Halloo! from me to thee.

Sombre in hate, clear-eyed, dawn-browed, a mock in thy soul,
A mock at psalter and sceptre and a sneer for the sickly old God
    in the temples of stone—
Hail! Cynic and Mocker of Nazareth: greeting from me to thee!

De Profundis

Night! Night Eternal Night, whose black vapors have filled all
        the sluiceways of Time—
Night! ageless and void, seamless and bald:
Night upgurgling from chaos,
Upswirl of the noumenal seas,
Drape me and veil me from the illusory lights of this world!

My being's at nadir,
I pass into my solstice,
I have touched of Its garment,
The black thing It weaves on Its sentient looms,
Its great blouse of black which encircles the world fold upon fold—
While we crawl in Its creases and guess.

Sit I in the night of Its sleeve,
Withering into eternities,
Bowed in Its night, in Its night!

On a Marriage

I hear laughter and there is a feasting, and another marriage is made—
A conspiracy has been formed to accouch another being.

Thou child unborn that now resteth in eternal day, day that is neither light nor dark;
Child that art yet uncreate and unwhipped of Pain,
In laughter and in feasting they have conspired against thy blissful sleep
There in the Unconscious,
There where thou art lapped and laved in non-being.
Hast thou heard the rumors from the lust-plane,
The guilty murmurings from the priest that made two beings incorporate?
Dost thou know thou art doomed to be born, to bear the cross and have the nails of pain cleave thy temples?

O thou sweet dweller in the White Temple,
Baby! Baby! as yet a lustful dream in two human hearts!
Already thy white robes are stained by a tiny red mark—
Thou art doomed to enter the lazar house.

Baby! Baby! I hear thee in the night weeping and wailing 'gainst thy birth:
For another marriage is made.

The Syncopated Spinner

Yon drowsing Spider that squats there upon Time's rotting timbers
Spinning her seven webs of a million threads,
Spinning and weaving from the birth of the Primitive Cycle—
Her criss-crosses, her mazes and labyrinths that are called
    Eternal Laws by the midges caught in the films
Spun by that drowsing Spider squat there upon Time's rotting
    timbers:
Awake! thou great spinning demon, shake webs and midge-men
    into the Nothing,
And with the shade of a smirk that I know resume thy loathsome
    pastime
There squat upon Time's rotting timbers!

Love and Sleep

I am a pale passionate Pilgrim evoked from the dust and the dark.
In my brain are the molten ivories of the dawn, in my heart the
    brooding desire for thee.

Whispers of the purple hours to come, whispers of the white
    eternities past,
Draw me hither and thither and nowhither.

Ah, me! shall I rest here awhile on the chubby round earth or
    travel back to the ivoried eternities?

Stand I thus at pause,
I, a pale passionate Pilgrim evoked from the dust and the dark.

The Watcher

Who are these shadows about me—my neighbors, my nearest,
>the jostler whom I felt at my elbow?
I—I who have gazed into the eternities and can in a glance pierce
>the curtains of Time,
Who have watched through this night the endless procession
>into being and beyond
(The cry in the womb, the release, the hasty scud across earth, the
>thud in the Pit!);
The screams in the dark, seen in a vision the Wheel go around
>and around
And the writhing, pain-gutted images clinging to the blood-
>smeared spokes—
I—what have I to do with this black, seething Now and its
>shadows?

Surge around me, ye humans, ye water-gymnasts;
The tide's running out, the present is ever-dissolving and the
>morn bringeth death to ye all.
But I who 'plash in the eternal waters and stray to the pallid
>horizon
Will return on the day of your silence, the Same, ever the Same!

Face to Face

It is well thou art hid, O Lord,
And sittest with glued lips fast on thy throne beyond the yellow
    disk of day.
Up from the slime I came, a Caliban blaspheming, leaning on
    crutch, superb hate in my eye,
Peering through bramble and forest for Thee.
Aeons ago was I thus, and now I am here, still evolving,
Planted firmly on two feet, almost at thy heels, not vexed, as
    cunning as thou,
O Lord of the vortices, fiend in the flux!

Linked to Prometheus, linked to great Lucifer,
I'll meet thee at the Great Crossways
And heal thee forever of the disease of creating.

My Shadows

Yonder lies my way.
Yea, I have taken the road, and in a sleep, in a cycle, I returned to
    the forks—
For all things are One, and beyond the One I cannot step.
The gad ever stings, and the Furies drive me forward—over suns,
    over flaming chaotic foreworlds,
To the hilt of creation;
But my thought is firm-set: illusive the flight, the return, the urge,
    the reaction.

I move not.
Based in the One, squatted here at the forks where the grooves of
    Change center,
I move not,
Adventure not forth,
Ran not that race over far-streaming worlds, nor danced on the
    cosmic pain-ladders.
'Twas my dominoed self,
An aspect of me, a shadow that travels forward and backward
    and upward and downward on Time's dirty screens.

What road shall I take when all things return unto me?—
I who move not on Time's dirty screens, was not touched by the
    gad;
I who am here at the forks where the grooves of Change center,
Who am One and the All, am motion and rest.

The Vigil

Here in the naked primal night,
Here where the Veiled sits graven in silence in Its garden of weeds,
Here where the Nothing drowses and mutters of a Something to
    come;
Here where the fangs of my soul have fastened at last;
Here where through wild-steaming streams of passion and great
    shroud-like dawns
I have dragged my undying Desire—
Here, too, will I vigil with Thee through the glutted eternities—
Thou imbecile artisan, thou bungler, evader, rhetor and faun!

The Closed Room

I am at the door of the Closed Room,
I stand without, whispering and chatting to myself, in many
 fantastic attitudes,
Like gnomes that skulk in castle-moats.
There are finger-marks on the door-knob—
Many, many have gone in, no one ever came out.
Through chinks I hear vague rumors, or is it the echo of the
 blood in my arteries?
And my eyes have spied, as I think, a light falling through cracks
 in the wall,
Or is it only the reflection of brain-sparks on the polished wood?
I finger the old worn knob, but am not yet admitted.

Half-Seen

Out from the brake and stubble of sense I peered for a moment—
Was that Thee that passed on the wind?
Once, too, I swam out beyond sight of all land and emerged on
    the crest of the highest wave
Was that Thee that sped over the horizon?
I throttled one by one each image in my brain on a night when
    the north-wind blew from the Zenith—
Was that Thee that startled me into a body again?
Ride thou on the wind, or merge in all horizons, Image
    unimaged,
Escape me Thou canst not, for I am the part that must make
    Thee whole at the last—
At the last!

The Long Vigil

Like sunlight, I touch all things, yet nothing do I gain;
I am neither richer nor poorer than I was at the beginning of
    things.
Passion, hope, pain, grief, leave me unchanged (I shed universes
    and moult cycles).
To the eye of the world I am tossed like a cork on rough waters,
But I know I have stood Here since the Day of the Primal
    Appearance,
Transfixed in supreme wonder,
Rigid in pride, dissenting, unmoved.

Prophetic

Time lies cataleptic in my brain:
Eternity alone reigns there.
Infinite space has shrunken to a single point of fire,
From whose heart radiate the trackless voids.

Life I have bosomed in a sigh.
I will exhale with the dawn,
Step lightly to my zenith,
Death in-wrapt.

Resurrection Night

I slept,
And out of their ancient tombs of tissue-plasm streamed a
    shadowy host of Living Dead.
Gliding silently across the waxed and shining floor of my soul,
They breathed their breaths upon the emptied mirror of my
    mind:
And Terror and Guilt captained that crew.

The subtle fingers of the dawn brushed my brow
And my soul flowed back into the sluiceways of the old familiar
    world;
But long I laid in wonder staring at the wall,
For in that night I had again become the Things I was before my
    birth.
And Terror and Guilt were old shapes of me.

BIRD OF THE NIGHT

O thou pinioned Thought,
Where wilt thou wing me to-night?
Dug from the marl and silt of my soul,
Breath of my delicate dreams,
Bird with the eyes of the circular fires
Sucked from the suns we have grazed in our flight,
Cleaver of lightnings,
Warbler in the zenith of my passionate being,
Plumed and feathered for thy mystic spiral progressions,
Where wilt thou bear me this night?

The Cleft In The Wall

They pass through my brain and leave not a mark:
Cities and women and autumnal skies.
I am related to nothing in the phenomenal flux,
The world-days are vain shapes of desire, a mist on my mirror, my
    mind—
My mind that reflects
Cities and women and autumnal skies,
Wrack of old Chaos, wrack of old Time.
My soul is a fountain that balances the ball of the visible cosmos;
I toss high, I toss hither and thither the whole universe, the
    hollow ball of desire—
It is nothing to me, a sport, a day-dream, as meaningless as old
    death and old birth,
Or cities and women and autumnal skies.

I travelled far with my pickaxe and spade and spied by chance a
    tiny cleft in Time's granite wall—
I called it the Now;
And through it I peeped like a boy through a knot hole,
Peeped into the Infinite,
A sea no bigger than a dewdrop, placid and waveless and spaceless.
(What Giant Shape lay therein,
The opening and shutting of whose eyes gendered immeasureable
    cycles?)
I passed through the cleft of the Now with infinite labor, and
    dispersed body and soul,
And cities and women and autumnal skies drift past my sight and
    leave me untouched.

The Truant

What was Its mandate?
Where is the script It placed in my hand?
Who sent me on this strange errand?
Or was it—No! No! too horrible!
And yet—and yet, how came I here?

In the immobile immensities,
Where renascence and decay and the plexed dream called Life
      were still unsensed—
Before I aggregated,
Before I anealed into an I,
Before the first stratum of lust was laid,
Before the dispart from the All—
In the immobile immensities something was ordered of me;
I was sent on an errand!

Hey ho! I have dallied with mortals too long,
Yet I dare not return without the thing done.
Or was it—No! No! too horrible!

Change and an Ending

Glow, glow, thou yellow fire, mother of me—
Thou shalt reclaim me body and soul.
Shine, shine, thou pulsing white eyes of the night—
I shall quiver in thy lights and be recompounded in thy crucibles
    of clay.
Moon! Moon! yellow-sick in amorous need of life, shall I not be
    as thee—
Still, cold and age-seamed?
Yea, in the whirl of the atoms and the swirl of great hidden forces
I shall be accouched in an uttermost star,
Builded anew in the dirt of a still unwombed world,
Speak, dream, languish and rot again and again,
Go the round of the infinite cycles till I spy, as by chance,
It, the Cagliostro, the Worker, the Kneader of mud-shapes,
Slay It there where I meet It,
And lay me down, out of Space, out of Time,
Certain of endless quiescence for me and for Thee.

The Quest in the Flesh

Here where the forces elemental circle me, caress me and touch
 my city-scattered parts to a whole;
Here on the mount, 'neath a blue-burnished heaven and a
 passionate luring sun,
Where the war of the wind with the leaves mocks at the strength
 we have hid;
Here is the lesson to learn, here is the Teacher eternal,
The war-lord of Space, the parent of hate and of love.
Do I not hate with a love that's intense?
Is not my soul strengthened in battle?
My brain is a duel of opposing forces,
And the thing that I war against is more precious to me than the
 tickle of grass or the ease that brings degradation.

War! War!—bring me helmet and shield and the sword of the
 spirit;
The great weaponed Self that I seek and that forever seeks me
Is shut in a tower of gold o'ergrown with weeds and the rank,
 poisonous fungi of outworn selves,
And here, gripped in these forces elemental,
I make a passionate compact with my dumb, brutish instincts
To assail every live-dead thing that hinders my march to that
 tower of gold,
O'ergrown, untended, unkenned;
And there in the winds, in a fury of battle, deliver the Self in the
 light of the sun—
Self that shall live to its uttermost transfigured instinct,
Self that am God of all gods.

In the Adytum

The door is ajar—
The door of my soul swung on the hinges of doubt;
It is ever ajar and waits for a Caller—
A Caller, in the night, or the day—I know not the time that he cometh,
Oh whether he cometh at all.
I crouch in my being, implacable, receptive, the ears of my soul in rigid prick;
Catching whiffs of the Verities borne from seas remote that mirror the catchpenny world in its depths.*
Sundered from all I sit,
To none abnegated,
Before my door standing ajar,
The door of my soul swung on the hinges of doubt.

What finger-marks these on the white knob of my door?
Narrow, black finger-prints, telltale of thinkers and ghosts,
Or maybe somnambules who have walked out of the world,
Or he, beloved of my soul: Has he called?—where loafed I then?
Who wills may enter,
But none have I seen—
Seen enter the door that's ajar,
The door of my soul swung on the hinges of doubt.

---

* The line "Catching whiffs..." was removed in the second edition of *The Shadow-Eater*.

The Way Out: Bio

Like a polished pearl hid in a pocket,
Like lighted tapirs set in the murk of a crypt,
Like the flicker of phosphor on dun seas,
Like a meteor athwart the heavens of Cimmeria—
So the Secret of my soul shines for me in this timeless Night.

Moth-Terror

I have killed the moth flying around my night-light; wingless and
    dead it lies upon the floor.
(O who will kill the great Time-Moth that eats holes in my soul
    and that burrows in and through my secretest veils!)
My will against its will, and no more will it fly at my night-light
    or be hidden behind the curtains that swing in the winds.
(But O who will shatter the Change-Moth that leaves me in
    rags—tattered old tapestries that swing in the winds, that
    blow out of Chaos!)

Night-Moth, Change-Moth, Time-Moth, eaters of dreams and
    of me!

My Holy Lust

The lust of the sailor for new lands,
The lust of the boat new-launched for the turbulent, foaming,
    sky-running waters—
Lust ever and ever I thus.
I stand in the ring of the earth and lust for the rings above and
    beyond
That widen into great monstrous nooses in the pits of azure and
    opal
Till my glance is lost in the fire-capped zenith—
Lust with my eyes and my ears, lascivious of all things unguessed,
    all things not conquered.
I lust for the Strength that runneth before
And purge myself of the close-clinging, stiffening muds of old
    custom,
Running the fine needle of my quickening Desire through a
    million ephemeral nuclei,
Thrust to the core of each vanishing truth.
My lusts hold me taut and redeem me of pain,
And I sigh and I sob and I laugh in the ear of the Loved One,
    spread on the winds, locked in the blast, till she yield and
    diswomb her last secret—
She, my finality, target of lusts, peeping here, peeping there, ever
    lost, ever gained—
I come at her again and again on the arrows of Time.

The Overone

The great God sleeps and dreams through Me,
And cycles run and cycles ebb
And still It blossoms in my brain
Or withers in my stoppages:
The God in chains,
The Ghost in leash to Me!

O sleep is deep,
And deeper still the unborn dream,
And under sleep there is a sleep
Where walks the great Noctambulist.
Bitten by the vermin host,
Stung by knout, gnawed by gad,
It flushes through my arteries,
The rising God,
The Coming One,
The God that's tethered in my brain!

The Ultimate

I wait for Thee in vile places a little while
And wait for Thee in high places a long while.
In the bellies of my adders I make my way laboriously,
And I am that high look-out in the eye of the eagle lost in the azure infinities.
Thy Secret, O universe, I have willed to know;
Thou swift-hurrying, invisible Spirit buried 'neath thy monstrous uncountable atoms—
Where will I fall flat upon Thee,
Weaving myself into Thee?
Flying to my remotest zeniths,
Diving far into the unplumbed Nothing,
Waddling in these earth-muds,
I seek Thee with my passionate intent Here
And in the mutable many Here-afters.

The Sleeper

My soul fell asleep, asleep in a great city, among the leering faces
    of her millions;
The iron hoofs of many strange and monstrous animals ground
    their imprint in my prescient white Self
That lay stark and helpless on the highways of the world:
O my Soul, my Soul, awake thou!

The waves have gone over me
And crawling things with fiery eyes have wriggled onto the white
    throne where I ruled,
And the old Seven Deadly Delights have kissed me each one
And licked up my strength with their smooth yellow tongues:
O my Soul, my Soul, awake thou!

O the terror of sleep and of Me who am blotted, erased and spun
Into things that are vile and gross.
And the long death of Me that drank of this hemlock of earth
    that brings not the death that is surcease—only a death of
    vile dreaming, a lapsing without a forgetting:
O my Soul, my Soul, awake thou!

Out of their crypts stalk my elder old selves,
And whilst I stare with the impotent eye set in the head of the
    dead
They drive in the little brass rivets of habit to the core of my
    being:
O my Soul, my Soul, awake thou!

The Alleys of Eld

Night and the Sea and the depths of Despair!
The gulfs of Time, the moaning of wastrel souls,
The ullulation of fiends in the brackish currents of Change:
I heard with an myriad Ear, and was withered and worn and
    wrenched in the screws.
How came I into the Alleys of Eld?

Endless doors were closing behind me—
I could not go back, the slams were decisive, I heard ITS skeleton-
    key turn in each lock,
And peering back, I looked into its eyes, sinister as Time's face,
    brooding upon me—
As I hurried down the Alleys of Eld.

A sudden emergence here on this shore,
My brain still gimletted with the memory of those eyes,
My ears still pricked with the click! click! of ITS skeleton-key—
Emerged! ah! the Night and the Sea and the depths of Despair
    and the memory of IT!—
Emerged from the Alleys of Eld!

Love the Destroyer

I reject Love—
Love and its sibillant, low-murmured lies, sweet sting of fair
    bodies, old meat of old Death.
The boom of the red sea of lust rings dull in my ear—I have seen
    the waves go over many; dead, dead forever they lie in the
    steaming hot currents that bubble up from the mud-beds.

I reject Love—
Love that has strewn millions of Me along the path I upclomb,
    shredded my flesh with its claws and burnt out my brains in
    its long searing clutch.
Through that ageless black night, with my earth-itch fair full
    upon me, once my Eye was stabbed by a bolt from the
    fulgurant Light and my soul pined away from its love and
    grew strong in its terrible Nay.

I reject Love—
Love that accouched every star in the blue, that with knout of
    Desire sends the young worlds grunting round and round
    the senescent suns.
I hear swash and lave of the unimagined fulgurant Light,
    burning sure and serene at the Axis of things—soft swash
    and soft lave wrought in the great Mnemonic Cell-Soul of
    me!

Rejection

The wafer of Time I have bitten—sweet it was not.

Each taper of thought stood at flare in my soul—and I saw only
    the density of the gloom.
My soul has fumed at the lips of Thy women.
(Pah! 'twas a fool's trick to try to seduce me the Hunter of Thee.)
Effort, emotion, thought, dream, lust—what have these for me?
I came to judge of Thy works, not to dance to Thy pipings.

Thou canst not stanch the woe that is mine,
Thou canst not bribe to sleep my Everlasting Nay.
Godlike am I in Thy presence,
As weary as Change, and as young;
A mendicant rebel, a Presage, a rejecter,
A contriver of strange things, unbegotten, eternal!

An abattoir hid in a garden of roses—
Such is Thy universe:
Thus do I judge!

The Spear of the Great Spurning

Upreared in the night, pallid-gray 'gainst the moon,
Towers she they call Astoreth, goddess of flesh and of worms,
Older than all years, younger than Love.
Alone I stand in that desert in that dead of the night
With the Spear of the Great Spurning, tipped with the poison of
    an Ageless Thought,
Leveled straight at her dugs.

Pallid-gray! Pallid-gray! 'gainst the moon, sick is young Astoreth,
    who saw me grow from cycle to cycle—
Astoreth pales 'gainst the moon at the vision of him who will not
    suck at her dugs.

Drive well, O Spear of the Great Spurning—
Drive well at the Mother of Life, who rowels our flesh—goddess
    of flesh and of worms!
Drive well, O Spear, tinct with my Thought!—
With her fall comes the Great Manumission, and nothing else
    shall be
Save the beat of my Thought in the Void.

NEW YORK CITY, 1902-1906.

THE SUBLIME BOY
(1926)

Resolved

I would not have him back.
He is wave and flame and crescent moon.
He is the bulging, westward-moving night,
The ivory lap and lave they call the dawn,
And he circles with the eagle round and roundabout Mont Blanc.

Uprendered

He is the slab of light across my door,
A signet set upon the brow of Time—
The Boy that was uprendered to the Light
And flung beyond the gates of Accident.

Unwithered

She sepulchred his soul in soft, lascivious flesh,
She gashed his mind with red and purple images,
She rabbled him with frantic, hot desires—
Then called to him from out the Ebon Gate
And with gesture nympholeptic locked him up between her
    breasts.

Waiting

You are not buried where your body lies,
Where Matter and the Worms hold long carouse;
But there, atop the catafalque of Night,
Where Aldebaran has sheened your soul in silver light,
You listen for the bugles of the Dawn,
The heralds of the promised Rendezvous!

Pre-Destined

With eye that cleft the many-colored Lure
And smote with godlike mock upon the face of Circumstance,
He plunged with ecstasy into his Dream,
Where now he lies slabbed up in silence.

Home

No more the fallacies of flesh,
Nor ever to drink in with sickening nostril
The stench of multiplied vain hopes,
Or be the hanger-on to Change,
Or play the bawd to concupiscent sense—
No more, and still no more forever! of these ancient, sweet
 seductions
For him who by a single, swift, inexorable act now reigns in
 Nullibiety.

IMMUNE

He stands a carven image in my brain, the great Hellenic frenzy
    in his eye,
And Time that sucks into her maw the Thee and Me and things
    not yet compounded
Shall touch him not! Shall touch him not!

ANATHEMA!
Litanies of Negation
(1928)

Anathema!
Litanies of Negation

I

I WILL break every web that is woven and spin my light and my night over the universe. I will shake down high towers of thought and lay belly wise over the Ark of the Covenant in sign of contempt.

I will rend for you the arras of illusion and show you your dreams and your lives and your dogmas under the aspect of Eternity.

And seeing this, you shall wither where you stand, and labor for breath, and your eyes shall mirage the tempests of Change.

II

THINK you an Idea slumbers in this eternal Becoming?

Think you there is a cream-nut in the husk of evil, a core of "redemption" in the apple of life?

The "far-off divine event," long and under many guises have you of this world been taught it!

Divine and fair it is—that final event: lights out through the Cosmos, the human a-bed forever and forever!

II

I AM the Illicit One. My liaisons with the Innominable have spawned the imps that work in the wainscoting of your beliefs, and I breathe decay upon the rafters of your House of Certainties while you lie sleeping in your bed of illusions.

I am the Illicit One, and my cabals were held in the damp air of the Ancient Morning, before the first cock-crow of human thought.

I am the Illicit One, myself a bastard of infinite Chance who may never occur again.

I sneer at you from the zenith of my knowledge and catch you, billion upon billion of earth-flies, in the net of my thought-strands.

There I smile at you, smile at you, with a smile frost-bitten in the boreal winds of the Infinite, a smile covered with the rime of my inexorable sneer.

Ah! The humor of circles and flies!

IV

You who are incarcerated in the finite and I who see you all in the mirror of Eternity; you who see each other as definite, palpable, familiar units, and I who see you under the aspects of Change, indefinite, impalpable, a stupendous unfamiliar repetition—do you know the terrors of this isolation, can you guess of the cold on these peaks where I have grown these bouquets of edelweiss that I bring to you down there in the mud-huts of belief?

Around the bivouacs of your beliefs and the night-fires of your sacred exaltations I pry and I skip, and from the recesses of my Beyond-World I hurl, ever and now, an arrow that rends your tents, O Philistia, and blenches your brows with the thought of me, the scorner of gods and of humans.

Could you fathom my contempt and my love for you, could you stand at the crossroads of the Expedient where I often stand, leaning on my wand of ebon—would you not then be like me? Would you not then strike tent and bivouac, no more at a Here or a There, and follow me, the gypsy of thought, the unhallowed trooper through Bad Lands and Good Lands, the implacable foe of all shelters?

But lacking humor and perspective, lacking the satanic instinct, you stick to your levels and straight lines, squat there in the morass of your beatified illusions; and it is well for you thus, you mudmoles—bait that you are on the hooks of my venomous pride!

V

I draw you forth from the scabbard of your familiar illusions, quiver and shriek as you may, and toss you into the miraculous light of the unknown and unknowable.

See you now the carnage of matter and mind they call Life? The unslaked thirst for being of the mystical Ghost of etheric climes you call God? The panorama of Change you call Progress? Ennui—the spawner of worlds? And the great flakes of pain that descend on the unimaginable generations of men like an everlasting black snow?

Then into your scabbards again, you dull, pointless ones; back to your cabals and cobwebs, you jailbirds of place, convicts of routine!

VI

I AM the acorn of evil and the millet-seed of the Eternal. I am Aphrodite that was and the Anti-God to be. I am the cornucopia of the concrete and the glowing crucible of all abstractions. I am the Fatal Appearance. I bring you salvation in a sneer.

I am the epiphany of Oblivion—I bring you the hemlock of quiet. Drink, you who are muzzled and leashed I move in the mystery of Light. You, planet-parasites, move in the mystery of my shadow, an incalculable throng on the web your lusts weave from generation to generation.

Shall I evoke for you the spasms of pain and the sobs of long-vanished worlds, all gathered here on my heart like the dents on a shield at a siege? Will you listen to the Symphony of the Nil? Ask rather for plague and rapine, you hedged and herded crew.

For I am the Beethoven of Negation!

VII

I AM a monochord and I strum the eternal Nothing. I am built of the overtones of mind and matter. All intelligence finally streams toward me, and the death-rattle of the last hope shall be muffled on my bosom.

You who stand over the trough of your instincts and fatten your eyes and your lips on the slops of this world, are you not nearly sated? Will you lap up the last shreds before listening to me and acclaiming my sneer?

The Ideal and the Real—at those troughs you have fed since Time spun its webs. You are held in the vise of opposites, and gods and demons are squeezed from your vent-holes, and under a million guises you fabricate the same and the same and the same.

I have selected you, microcosms of clay, to be my butts. It is against you I hurl my inextinguishable laughter, for I am the intangible point of your every perspective, the piston-rod of your motions, the humorous imp of chagrin secreted at the core of your hopes.

From the discord of your lives I have extracted the harmonies of negation. Out of jangle I have constructed the melodies of discord.

I bring you funeral plumes plucked from the catafalques of ancient cycles of life, now rigid in nullibiety.

Let us wear them for boutonnières to celebrate the defeats of this day and the disasters of multiple morrows.

And I will assemble before you the Bacchic Chorus of Negation—Sophocles and Lucretius, Gautama and Schopenhauer, and Leopardi and Baudelaire—the Bacchic Chorus of Negation, I say, for they found an exquisite joy in their Nada! and spit from the height of their pride on the world, and grew drunk on a vintage headier than Hope.

VIII

I FLOAT before your eyes now like a vapor, a mixture of the unimaginable Ideal and the Baleful Vision.

I am an alloy. Into me has passed all the dreams of the ages. I am the apocalypse of the thing you fear.

I am compounded of you all—you my larvæ—and I wing away into the wells of light—I, taster of all honeys and nectars, quaffer of all poisons, breeder of venoms, with antenna that reach to the navel of the unborn.

With you I have labored through the Unconscious, through the waste-matter of worlds and forms, evolving the eternal Illusion— we the tools and the scaffolding, the elaborate experiment in Time of a God sick of his error, who struggles up through the morass of our souls to the citadel of our final negation.

IX

YOU have sowed these myriad of æons in the furrows of the Future, and what have you gathered but thorns and thistles that you weave into crowns?

You have woven these uncountable ages on the looms of your hopes, and do you weave else but your winding-sheets?

Fallow is the glebe of this world, and the shuttles of desire are haunted by pixies of deft cunningness, and you sow and you weave to no ends.

Out of the miraculous tomb of the past issue the epiphanies of your countless to-morrows, which in turn become corpses. And still, you paid pimps of the old whore Hope, watch at that door, though I have told you again and again that it is only the trick-cabinet of the Master—I the implacable watcher and challenger who loves and sneers at you from his zenith of Knowledge.

X

I WAR more on the errors called truths than on the truths that you call errors. Your vices to me are more beautiful than your virtues.

Not until you are nude to the soul will I take you up into my frozen heavens.

Not until you class all truth with all error does freedom dawn in your souls.

Not until you have broken out of all tombs will I show you the irony of God.

Of me Pride has made its lordliest victim; but inasmuch as I sneer at myself and guffaw at my insight am I master of my Pride, for only Pride kills Pride.

Laugh upon laugh I launch at myself, and when you are with me in the zenith of my frozen heavens you will see me scourging myself with the whips of self-mockery.

The pride of the Nihilist! I am trapped like you all tombed in the belly of self.

XI

I WILL muffle the gods in sleep and house myself in an acorn which shall be eternally sterile.

All gods will I turn into shadow—Apollo and the Overman to come no less.

From surface to surface, from unity to unity, I shall grow, incorporating in myself things that were and things that are.

All unities are complexities, all complexities are infinite unities. The Infinite itself—the dearest illusion of my brain, the Infinite, my spiritual itch!—shall die unto me like a shadow lost in a sea. For I am the Super-Infinite.

Where I am there shall be Nothing; where Nothing reigns there I shall be.

Circle on circle, arch on arch, span on span, cosmos on cosmos—they are nothing in my apprehension, and a single flash of a firefly is as much as the light of all suns, and the croak of a frog in a pond is the measure of all human sound that has been.

One said he had been rowed and ferried through Chaos. Another said he preached the Beyond-Man. I say I am the Chaos through which he was rowed and ferried and I am that Beyond-Man. And

I say that both Chaos and Beyond-Man are the illusions of sleep-walkers.

The pride of direction in our sacrosanct seers! The vanity of origin, the vanity of end! Their tongues babble like fishwomen. I wind up their dreams on the reel of my Insight.

What mansions they build—these prophets and poets and babblers of futurity!—all at last blown to atoms in the powder-house fixed on my shoulders.

XII

I HAVE had lewd intercourse with the Shapeless. I have basked in the ironic glints that fell from Its unperceived eyes.

He who is the magnet of all unities shall be the temple of all discords.

I am the Mecca of all sorrows, the blenched and frozen cheek on which all tears fall, the Night unto which all secret sighs are uttered—yet am I a Mansion of Revels, a Hall of Laughing Echoes.

I am the Mirthful Prometheus. When I have swallowed the last shred of the Infinite, I shall found in my Void the Dynasty of Laughter—laughter silent, ironic, dissolving myself in its sterile ripples.

Little brittle souls of earth—all you who come and go, spawn of worm and ape—you will be there with me, soul of my soul, bowels of my bowels!

XIII

THIS pastoral I pipe for you, O Philistia!—sweet fetor at my banquets, bouquet from my cesspool. Suck I not venom from your breath like a stealthy cat in the night? Are you not civet and musk in my bedclothes?

"Vox populi, vox Dei!" How well I know *that*! Shadow of the Bungler thou art, O people—the crutch of the Blind One.

With a spring and a smirk I am among you, winding in and out among your tents, O Philistia; and you draw aside as from a leper, a leper with cowl and lazarus-bell. And I pass on into the desert and am blent with its sands and lost in its purple shadows.

For truly am I a leper in your sight. Touch but my garment of black and you will be infected with thought, and through all your white tents will stalk my Black Death: my cosmical insight, my petrifying Super-Infinity.

I am a hangman and gravedigger. I shall wrap you all in a shroud no bigger than the wing of a day-fly, yet you shall be housed in the Super-Infinite, for large and small I know not.

All illusions swing like decayed corpses from the gibbet of my Insight. I peel off the wrappings of hope yard upon yard till the mummified Nothing starts from its nakedness. For, at last, you are wrappings, older than time, that enswaddle me—the uncreate Nil.

XIV

I DANCE upon the catafalques of all my dreams, become the chrysalis of fairer dreams, and emerge into my super-nothingness to become the fixed and hollow eye of Truth.

The water goes over the fall and the sun slants upon the crag, but still am I fixed in my Nothingness.

And the gods awake again, casting their filaments into the winds of the morn, and new human cycles bubble out of their mouths—but still do I keep my Nothingness.

Eden-trees blossom again, and Eves come forth from their lairs, and a myriad Christs tell their doleful tales and stagger up their Calvaries but forever keep I my rigidity.

The feudal chiefs of philosophy come unto me and find in me a sacrament of conciliation. Only those by Ganges and Brahmapootra have dreamed aright, only they have guessed me.

Epicurean and ascetic, idealist and realist, pagan and Christian are eclipsed in my penumbra, the veritable shadow of the Super-Infinite.

I trumpet beyond all suns and finger the flute of Time, swimming the rapids of all conceivable lusts, gayly dashing my brains out again and again on the reefs in the whirlpool. They are my pas- times. No hap can come to Nothingness.

I slake my thirst at many wells, and fard my face with lies, and appear as Man; or turn hypocrite, and thus become God, and tweak your brains with fair infinite vistas.

XV

I HAVE clogged their brains with images and set them at the goalposts of life and sped with them along their road until the little hole was reached wherein they tumbled, and I sealed them up with slabs of ice.

O Poet, hast thou seen my footprints—there on the hillock of your loftiest imagining? Have you seen spoor of me, O Philosopher, in your profoundest meditations? Have you guessed that the undertaker of the Infinite, God's gravedigger, passed your way?

Time and Change and Matter, those bastards of infinite shapes, are dungeoned in me, and Eternity is only one of my peepholes.

Glance through your telescopes, strain through your microscopes—all that you see, sublime and wondrous in your sight, are only fungi on my breast.

Destruction, creation—what names! I am the Great Necromancer. Destruction and creation—to me—are merely ingredients.

I reverse all axioms. Out of nothing comes something, as a god is born of the air; out of something comes nothing, as all things return to me.

With the yardstick of their logic they measure the All! Buzz, little gnats of my noon; buzz out your systems here on my eyelash—sometimes I drowse and allow you to rest there and buzz.

XVI

How many times have I suspended my audience in the kingdoms of sentiency! In my anterooms and festal halls they awaited me— they the helots of Chance, the parvenus of accident. But I stayed within, interred in my thought.

They hallooed to me from without, hurling stones through my windows—sons of carpenters, fauns and nymphs, a troop from Olympus, Bacchus and Venus, Priapus and Momus, all seeking to claim me the unfettered supergod. But I was fishing from the wharves of eternity with bait cut from my brain.

And from the depths of my impenetrable retreat I heard them go away singing, the carpenter's son singing the most laughable ditty of all.

But you shall not be lost, O pale gods and riant gods and prophets with the ludicrous symbols, for with natrum and oils I will embalm you forever in my funeral parlors and you shall gossip one to the other in my catacombs in another Thebes by another Nile.

For all gods and all saviors pass over my thought like the flying butt of a cloud over the blue of the firmament.

Like that mountain near ancient Thebes where were buried kings and servitors and which bulges with its dead, so have I millions buried in me, am a necropolis of ghosts, a living mausoleum of human vanities—all housed and hearsed in me.

XVII

I WALK through the woods flecked with the gold-leaf of noontime, drowsy with whispers, and the oaks bend to me, and the birds call to me (or is it I who chant gayly from their throats?).

I dandle the sea on my knee and allow it to slap me in the face with its foam as one allows a child so to do. It knows me, the space-eater, menstruum of time, avatar of the Inscrutable.

Or I leap on the back of the eagle, and when it has carried me to the confines of space I spring from its back and lave in the light of dimensionless suns.

Thus do I sport in the hippodrome of the Cosmos, drinking sometimes at the founts of the finite, lounging through the Louvres of creation, sometimes at watch from the eye of the Sphinx, or nonchalantly watching the hens warm me out of an egg. For verily I am a sportsman.

I am the rendezvous of the dead and the living. I am the trysting-place of those two lovers-in-secret, God and Lucifer. I am the clandestine meeting-place of all contrarieties.

Thoughts cling like leeches to my brain—that brain that is an eagle's nest hung on the edge of precipitous voids.

My thoughts are rungs in a ladder built in the air and which disappear in the non-existent.

When I am unapparent I am seen most; when I am abdicate 'tis then I reign. When I laugh you shall think I am weeping; when I weep you shall hear a guffaw.

XVIII

MY DREAM! What has it been? To baffle the sunlight, and stay the night, and raise the gonfalons of negation on the time-wide debris of men's hopes, and lead the planets, unshriven, to my abattoir of eternities—there over the Borderland.

I have ransacked each atom seeking a Purpose, have raked down the fires in uncountable suns, seeking in their ashes the secret of their flames, blended my souls with the translunar ethers, seeking to come full upon It. Only to find that I was atom and sun and ether and the secret thereof, the Anonymous It, the wellspring of the existent, the final tabula rasa!

XIX

MEN have been who have said they were the God-incarnate. Were they no more than that?

One said he was the Son of God.

I say God is my Son.

Like a ghoul, I prowl over the battlefield where lie a-rot my dead selves, and many a gem I rip from that rottenness, many a burnished sabre I pluck from its scabbard.

And over the graves of my accoutred selves grows the edelweiss.

XX

I AM the Present, and I hold all the Past as booty. I have pillaged the Future, and am the very core of the coming event.

In the Infinite, Nothing changes; in the Super-Infinite, Nothing is.

XXI

THERE is no one thing better than any other thing; there is no God greater than any other God. All are out of the dugs of Ennui—all makeshifts, spawn of fear and bad dreams.

Ideas are my concubines, sport of a day; then I breathe my disgust over their faces and they wither and pass into smoke.

To the Naught alone am I faithful—I the spouse of the Arch-Nothing—I the port and the haven of suns.

I have an inerasable kiss-print on my neck put there by Aphrodite, and a glittering brand on my forehead carved there by Lucifer, the Rightful Heir to the Throne.

Or did I put both marks there myself? For once I was born of the sea, and once did I sound fanfare of revolt in the Heaven of the Philistine Boaster.

I am the mystery of memory and the puzzle of laughter and the stretched bow of expectancy and the rubescent stem of passion.

XXII

IN ASHY regions of the sky I bare my soul to its latter nudeness and cross the portal-gate of the unimaginable Zenith and confront the Host in his turret.

There is parley and expostulation. For this and that we lash each other, he proclaiming, I denying, each standing stark in the other's eye, there in that mystic turret at the Zenith.

I came back to sentiency strangled with laughter—my boreal laughter, laughter that is like the frozen sunlight at the poles of the moon.

What things I beheld at that Zenith, what ludicrous jargon from the tongue of that doddering old Demiurge squat in his turret!—

He the asp of the cosmos, and I the dragon that swallows the asp. He the God of the living, and I the alembic of living and dead!

XXIII

IN THE souls of men I shall leave my heel-print, ghostly, ineffaceable.

In their hearts, those claviers of pain, shall be heard forever the buzz and hum of my negations.

XXIV

I AM the mirthful outlaw. Through my grin you may know me, and when you hear my peals of laughter in the night rise and bolt the door, for I tread at your sill.

I laugh till I reel, and I scoff at your God, O butter-lipped, simpering Philistia!

Jezebel, Messalina, Delilah, Thaïs, Aspasia and Laïs I unleash with a laugh and bid them run wild 'mongst your tents, while I caper in motley and jig to my mirth just to see your lickerish looks and the spittle flow from your lecherous lips.

Softer than all your dreams is my Néant, and you of the earth who seek forever an Elsewhere shall find it in my breast of ice.

XXV

HUMANITY wears my cast-off clothes, and I mask the gods as I will.

Ormuzd and Ahriman, Apollo and Maya, Christ and Wotan—they are only visible in the spotlight of my satiric smile.

XXVI

MY SOUL today is a butterfly with 'wildering wings and I have lain dormant on strange walls.

Last night I was a bat and was born of a man as he died. Tomorrow I shall be the hieroglyphic eye of a new-born child. Some days I am a gnat stinging the gods to a frenzy of destruction, and in sinister twilights I camp in the shadows and bivouac with elves.

I am the background of your dreams and the patina on your images. I am the salt in your tears and the reservation in your laughter, the mud-imbedded anchor of your doubts and the ennui that bases your happiness.

Of laughter I have strangled many times. I, too, died at Salamis, at Blenheim, at Verdun—died of the mirth that was in me when I saw the knight-errants of the Ideal fall under their banners scrawled with symbol of this and that, mouthing of God and of country.

The splendor of Northern nights lies in the winter of my eye as the aurora borealis flames over the Arctic wilderness. And if I am a Blind Pocket, then must you venture in, for there you will gather precious gems.

XXVII

I WILL reduce you and all worlds to cinders and ashes and make of the débris pale beams to illumine my eternal night.

I am out of date, being dateless. I am old-fashioned, being primordial. I am homeless, being from Nowhere. I am a nomad, living at all points of the compass.

The Super-Infinite welcomed me as a refugee from the tyranny of Time. I was postilion in the car of the devildare gods, and was mothered on the fiery breasts of comets. All these I spurned, for in my heart was nostalgia of the Néant.

I am mankind's valet, arranging his bib in the cradle, laying out his coffin-clothes on the day of his death.

I am Life's perpetual shadow, the eternal spirit of negation and denial, sucking through an invisible hole in the rind of your hopes the juices of joy.

Not until you lose your centre are you free, not until the axis on which you turn has split will you emerge from the Wheel, not until you take from your eyes the bandage that unifies all your dreams and acts will you be ready to take my hand and enter into my Ubiquity.

You shall be Puck and Belial, the spirit of helter-skelter, a will-o'-the-wisp from the Abyss, Mumbo-Jumbo, dryad and pixy—the veritable Deus ex Machina of the Puppet-Show.

And I will crown you with my black burnoose, which will flap in the tempests of our laughter.

XXVIII

SOMETIMES stretched dreamless in my Nowhere there come to me vague murmurs from a Beyond. I lie puzzled and pallid at *that*. Can there be, then, a Super-Naught unguessed of me?

Puzzled and pallid, lying a-dream in my Nowhere, these mysterious whispers come to me. Am I within earshot of my Co-Eternal? Is the Petrified One taking on godhood again? Is the Great Somnambule walking again?

XXIX

THE HOURS come dancing toward me arrayed in the purple of purpose, diademed with opals of hope, and they fade 'gainst my Doubt like sun- beams that fall into canyons.

I am a marble column veined with memories, pedestalled in the mists of Oblivion, crowned in the zenith with a gigantic Chimera.

My altars of iron are aflame with the dead—the dreaming and procreating old egos that infested my multiple selves that I plucked from their soft beds of pleasure in the heyday of their virility.

Into the braziers of Change I thrust them, and the smoke curls away in the winds, plucking at space, still seeking entity.

A funeral torch set over the cinders of my ancient abodes—such is my Thought, my last Thought, my immutable Dream.

XXX

AT THE cradle stands Hope, with seven paste stars in her hair, her lips rouged with the blood of her multiple victims, and over the whimpering eye of the newborn she draws the eyelid of illusion.

The first of all midwives I call her. She stood at the matrix of worlds and assisted at the birth of all lies. Antidote to the worm, wardrobe-mistress of all earth-pantomimists, high priestess who croons her incantations from the sloughs of failure—she reigns for her short eternity, to be finally engulfed in my Nada.

XXXI

I AM the first-born of Silence, the menacing white-cap on the horizon of your tenderest dream. I hang from the borders of tempests, and you have guessed something of me at the moment of death.

Eternal Expectancy with libidinous look and sumptuous lips, I come to expunge you and your brats.

Like a fox, I prowl around the sheepfolds of Philistia, carrying off the youngest to my burrow, teaching them the slyness of me.

There they are crowned with my sinister nimbus, taught the litanies of my Everlasting Nay, shorn of their fleece and stood naked where the hail from my heavens may slash at their flesh.

XXXII

High over the world and its débris of thought float my black emblems from their invisible halyards.

And there beyond emblem and halyard I rise and fall in the ether, splashing my well-beloved with spray from my dreams, building my echoes in their hearts, touching lightly with my finger their foreheads, the white screen of their thoughts.

XXXIII

Shall I break the seals on the tombs of your souls, shall I roll away the stones from the sepulchres of your griefs? Shall I draw you forth from the sack of identity and set you quivering on the threshold of my Super-Infinite?

Your souls will evaporate under my look, the close-knit pebble of identity disintegrate atom by atom in the breaking surf of my thought—surf of a sea that never spits up its dead.

I am the purple mountain which you will never reach. I am the horizon which you will never cross. I am the thought which you will never think. I am the sun whose setting you will never see.

XXXIV

The sterile sun of negation has reached its meridian. Strain your ear in the wind—Time itself is asking the hour of me!

Philosophers, pedants, prophets with their curious nicknames come to the outposts of their guesses like a caterpillar that crawls to the edge of its leaf.

Shined in pride, they walk past the forbidden and fall into the folds of my laughter, and will be rendered back to the earth—when I will—when I will!

XXXV

My dreams are black flowers that hang from the pale-green stems of my passion. Come you to browse in the garden? Beware of my black blossoms, O mules, O cows, O swine!

Where do I hide myself? In the light! In the light! And when will I be announced? When the final Light falls on the starfields of Lyra.

XXXVI

I AM a hell that is tired of flame, a heaven that is tired of joy, an Olympus stripped of its gods. I am a pagan who spits out the grape, a Christian who spits at the cross, and—most unbelievable of all paradoxes!—a Jew who spits on the Golden Calf!

XXXVII

TONIGHT I am an urn wherein lie the cinders of light. Can you read the inscription? It is a frivolous one. It is in memory of the pranks of a mocker for I have grown quite serious, become one of the people, and orbit from belly to genitals.

Super-Infinite! My Néant! My protean escapades! What balderdash, blasphemies, drivel is this! Come, thou Philistine Venus, breedy, swarming with brats! Come, thou middle-class Aphrodite, I am in love with thy sadic chastity and thy Christianized sighs and thy anaemic, respectable buttocks.

And so I am redeemed, come back to the old beaten track, sanctified in the sweat of her body, a perfect stench of moral uprightness.

XXXVIII

I SIT with my Sorrow and exchange silences with it—that unsurfeited Sorrow that sucks at the heart of the world.

Evening came to me at noon, and its chill wind blew the flowers I had gathered out of my hand and set upon my brow a coronet of shadows.

At the time when the thrush was singing in the brake it fell upon me and felled me with its dreaded kiss.

Then in my youth, when Cupid lay in ambush behind each star, the purple arrow crashed through my heart—I the picked target of that predestined arrow from the quiver of Proserpina.

And a cowled Thing handed me the keys of a certain hell, and another Thing whose feet were shod in lead and whose forehead was a wrinkled grin gave me the password to the dungeons of grief.

And being thus parcelled among them, I went forth. And I went forth, I say, being thus chosen.

XXXIX

I AM evolution accomplished, the end of the road, the final

negation that all affirmations mask; the heart of man's Dream; the underneath of all seeming.

I am Purpose abridged and Eternity curtailed; and from my child lips already there issued the lattermost sigh of expiring Mind.

I lie in rigid ambush behind my haphazard egos, and on the shuttle of my moods I spin my contradictory selves.

Destiny shrouds my movements in its shadows, and streamers of night unfurl from my shoulders and carry me over the borders of space.

I stand point-blank facing Eternity, forever the contemporary of Death, forever a hatcher and breeder of life.

And on the dark background of Time I engrave the destinies of races to be and efface the ancient equations and mark out the paths of the futile, ephemeral gods to come.

Sad heart of God, sad heart of Satan, I will pile up the days over your heads till the end of my whim, and then immerse you in my shadow.

The blood of the world has dried on my breast, and I am the red image of Evil, the imago of Pain, the eucharistic Pity.

I dream nebulous dreams, and they congeal and become life. I weep, and my tears drop in the furrows of the great trackless Void—seed of all griefs, poisonous kernel of all hopes.

Nothing was when I came; Nothing shall be when I leave. I am the dawnless tomorrow; the Mist wherein Memory is drowned; the outpost of Becoming; the stake and the goal of atom and God.

Life is the mask of Oblivion made fast to that invisible face with the golden threads of hope.

That mask was forged on an anvil of bronze by the old blacksmith, Necessity; and on that mask I am writ as a wrinkle that furrows the brow; or, again, you may find me in the deadly ironic line pencilled at the end of the lip.

Each one dwells in the tent of iron which he calls his ego, tent without chink, tent without slit, tent with its stake-poles driven into the depths—tent which I summon back to its ancient invisibility, splitting the ridge-pole of pride, laughing at what you thought should stand there forever—tent without chink!—tent without slit!

Let the desert keep its secret, and the Lord keep his counsel, and let them who sleep in the glacial mists of death guard their tongues. Before they were I was. On me all palimpsests are written.

Write what you may, whisper what you will—you write on the scroll of my being, you whisper into my ear.

XL

I AM the navel of Oblivion and the eater of shadows and Time's eternal vibration. Where there is shadow I am light; where there is light I am shadow.

The Archangel of Despair, the redemptive ironic Eye of Hope, the gibbet whence swing all my apostles—can there be death for me? Is there a shroud that can cover my spaceless soul?

I stretch my ivory limbs in the marble sarcophagus of memory and resurrect as I weave my eternities. To me the future is already obsolescent, and yesterday is the bud of which I am the immortal flower.

Hope is a dawn that never gives birth to a sun—give men that as a message.

XLI

HAVE you peered into the mysterious hells of infinite Apprehension? My flesh is a porous gauze which veils magical dreams and fiery abysses.

I quaff great flagons of light from unimaged goblets. Only Death understands me, only Death and she of the twin-black lights, she through whose nature I am woven and into whose monstrance I spill my dreams, she who pinions me to her wide and wondrous lips.

I unwind her soul-filaments and bind them 'round me in great bands of love—Infinite enmeshed in Infinite, the Holy Ghost sunk deep in his chosen Virgin.

We weave, one into the other, like sun-cloud into sun-cloud, softly, passionately; there is never an end; each center begets another center, and the hours are only shadows that crumble into the days that perpetually lapse and are lost in our blasting ecstasy.

XLII

My brain is a marvellous silk-worm which spins universes that are tomorrowless and unbegotten in any year. There are blazoned 'gainst it strange gleams from exotic moods; I listen to the beck and call of imperious atavistic visions, the suddenly illuminated memorabilia graven on the parchment of ancient emotions.

It is in the soundless beat of thought that I embosom God, the sombre ancestor of Hell, the seducer to all decoy-heavens; and it is there that I pull away the centerpole of relativity that holds up the tent of the Absolute and am the discarnate and unsocketted Eye that sees naught but the humanly unimaginable. The muffled dithyrambs of change tenant my ear, and I have memories that were recruited in Oblivion.

My brain is a monstrous chameleon lodged in a skull.

I am a sheaf of immemorial yesterdays, the bleeding adversary of my ancestors, the cradle of a spent world.

XLIII

The years have lived in my memory like a nest of tarantulas. The eternal was only the tremendous sweep of an invisible thought. My dreams, my early dreams, lied like the morning. I stand upright, rigid, in this tiny corner of the Cosmos, clamped in the black armor of melancholy.

I peopled the realm of abstract Time with an infinite number of despotic minutes, each one the tiny catafalque of a dead impulse, and lived in the marvellous enchantment of vengeful dreams.

I am an anvil, and when the mighty sledgehammer of fatality descends on me I tremble and totter—but also rise in a shower of flames into the azure.

I am without rhyme. I am without reason. I am without sense. I am without commonsense. I am. I was. I will be. I see.

XLIV

The atoms that make up men and mountains and heavens and suns each burst into a tiny flame and I led them at the windless hour to the very cope of Time and stood at the precipice of the Last Day. And one by one they guttered out, and I stepped into Eternity.

But I have fallen back into Time. Time—the dungeon of Titans.

Who shall add a cubit to the Infinite and a minute to Eternity? I do in the simple utterance I AM!

I have lived with kings and ancient gods and the couriers of fatality and the announcers of Life and Death and outstrip them all in my panoramic vision of Time. My flights into the light have been beyond light and I am pregnant with my selves.

My vision cannot take on matter. I am neither sculptor, nor poet, nor musician, nor architect, nor philosopher. My life is an image in a revery, and sense cannot coop what I see, nor can the atom, which is the ovary of the material, condense my infinitely fused parts.

The body, that trough of flesh wherein Time's muzzle ferrets and fishes and rends—I am not that. The frozen sun of Reason—I am not that.

The opaque center of universal light—I am not that. The godhead of Good—I am not that, nor the passionate heart of Pleasure. I am the mystery and the wonder-well of the Now, the fabulous Eye without a face, the millennium of Change.

XLV

AND THAT other God that I met on the way!

In his eyes were strangled thunders and frozen lightnings, and Prophecy was in his tongue.

He held a torch in his hand which burnt up suns.

The soul of that divine incendiary rose like a gigantic wave to a wondrous height and split against the cope of heaven and sprayed the constellations with miraculous fire.

XLVI

SOME days my thoughts are like lizards that lie motionless on the walls of my brain, stupefied by light. There are then no images that can contain my spectral intuitions, no words that can entomb my images, no ether that can transmit the light from that nebulous beyond-world.

Today, like a God, I fill the spaces of my brain with worlds, and they whirl on the ecliptic of the Infinite, brigands of space, spheres chiselled in canyons of light, globes sculpt in protoplasmic yesterdays.

I am the First Star of Heaven, and I shot my light into the passive, waiting spaces on the bridal night of the Universe.

Out of my tempest a song, out of my hell a Sphinx, out of my dreams an Eden, out of my desert a mirage of granite and gold.

XLVII

An invisible Thing enmeshes my soul, a monstrous Entity reigns in my being. I am bathed and enswathed in Silence, the silence of atoms, the silence of stars, the silence of ether, the silence of eternal, redundant generations, the silence of my invincible Self.

One thing has been since the beginning of Time: Silence. Who can be heard in the Infinite? What word will resound through Eternity? Who will fix a tongue in the throat of the Innominable?

Time hangs like a woman's hair over all essences and obscures the Unity that men seek to clasp. And dreams are dew on the leaves of rank weeds and the black plume of Death waves from each star.

Breast to breast with my Thought, I ride beyond Time and dreams and black-plumed star.

XLVIII

My soul is a planet, and I spin rings like old Saturn. Innermost ring, thou art my body; outermost ring, thou art the Infinite. Between them lie all comprehensible measurables—deserts and cities, ant-heaps and moons, men and Himalayas.

I spin Love, Power, Liberty, Irony, the four wombs of life—and the monstrous white ring of frost-bitten dreams is one of my circumferences.

I spin death, the sleeping-room without a clock; I spin the naked glory of her eyes in the penetralia of my imagination, and I spin the ring of reticence that girdles the Almighty Symmetry.

XLVIX

Each time my soul hatches a thought a new world is born, and from the nests of Memory I let loose the doves and ravens of my yesterdays to fly against the walls of fiery suns or to fall into the soundless reaches of my unremembered lives.

When the lightnings of my Thought illumine the sockets of my soul the clarions of the Future are muted and I stretch from nadir to zenith chiselled in fire—a glittering dagger that lies buried to the hilt in the bowels of the Dark.

I am a monstrous wave that seeks to splash the suns and toss my spray against Arcturus, and if I rise to calamitous heights it is that

I may fall back and sink into the depths of the Sea and slumber on the red coral isles of her heart.

L

THAT ELDER year! That elder year! Where is it gone? That ancient time when I was voiceless in the Infinite, when I was eyeless in the light, and when I knew not the swollen might of the Bud that could not blossom—where is it gone?

That year, like a white star, has faded in the conflagration of my images. I stalked through Hell with the assurance of Famine, and I would have raised my rebel standard on the moon and called upon the constellations for recruits. I am the Past, yet I cannot resurrect that year that lies imbedded in Time's marvellous frostwork.

In that elder time one thought remained in my head and reared itself like a single gigantic tooth in an empty mouth, a living full-fleshed thought pedestalled on a heart of granite. And now it lies embalmed in acid—for I have done with thought.

LI

I PUT my soul into the thing that passes, for only that which is transitory is everlasting. Spin and weave with the threads of desire thy impossible heavens and deceitful perspectives, O Maya! In the whirlwind of atoms and the tempest of images I am untouched, and in the frenzies of change I am the Changeless.

Only that which perpetually dies is immortal.

Precious is that which dies! Precious is that which lives for a minute! Precious is that which flies and deceives! Precious, thrice precious, art thou, Gypsy of star-lanes, mighty Itinerant, Troubadour, vagabond Spirit of spirits.

Precious am I in the sight of myself on the days I unlock the bolts of the Temple and exchange the dead lies of today for the beautiful lies of tomorrow!

Wild pulse of love, purple dreams of God, wistful faces that screen the ecstasies of memory, all things that hurry and all things that shimmer and fade are immortal in their time and matrixed in their beauty.

I am Transition—diaphanous, transfigurating, chimerical. I am perpetual in my nothingness, perpetual in my reality. I am color and light and motion, the retina of consciousness, the lying horizon of your nadir and zenith.

LII

I MEASURE Time by the number of eternities I have lived. Wastrel soul!

I measure Space by the number of infinities I have recorded. Spaceless soul!

My mind is the atlas of the spiritual world. Expatriate soul!

Karma may transform me, but cannot change me. Immutable soul!

The threads of my heart trail from far-away heavens and remote hells. O'er-laden soul!

LIII

I AM the Golden Law of Pythagoras and the cataleptic smile of Spinoza.

I am Progress with chimera in its eye.

I am the pendant lips of Pleasure and the epaulettes of Pride.

My imagination is a pharmacopæia of every sin.

My body has been strumpet and martyr and the manger of titans and saviors.

And my dimensionless Eye of azure and porcelain is shot with the blood in which all life bathes.

LIV

FROM the barricade of the Perpetual Revolution I proclaim my militant Dream.

Suffer liars and sinners and trespassers and outlaws to come unto me, and in their hands I will put a flaming sword and into their brains I will inject the brains of Prometheus, Cain, Siegfried and Don Juan.

And I will teach them newer and diviner trespasses that are yet but nebulous in the consuming light of my Consciousness.

And those that are weary and heavy-laden I will teach the wild music of my seditious passions, and they shall go forth restored from the celestial purgatories of my mind.

I shall know your greatness by your transgressions, and your littleness by your compliances, and your title to divinity by the blood on your fingers.

LV

I GIVE these thoughts of flame and ice to those who never will be born, to that impossible posterity that will never find its earthly womb, to that magical generation that will never be, to that sublime race of mortals who will ever remain faint shadows in the pool of my revery.

In the spiral nebulæ of space where colossal constellations await the seed of Time to hurtle into the ether; in the nebula of the subconscious where shadowy tomorrows laden with rich red seed of dream await their hour of exit; in the quarries of unimaged and dreamless silences, where the noiseless chisel of a ghostly Angelo is shaping out my destinies; in the microscopic universes latent in my blood—my posterity that never can be born look at me with the passionless eyes of the immortal and the dead.

Blear memories and hallucinating tomorrows come not to them, nor shall their souls turn throughout an eternity on the noiseless axles of Change, nor shall they clamber from star to star on the iron rungs of Karma, but, as antique as Oblivion, they lie stretched in the depth of a Lethe that threads its way where Time and Space are aliens.

These thoughts of flame and ice I give to them, that impossible posterity, who reign in the interregnums of Time and who perpetually usurp the throne of my soul in the royal succession of days.

LVI

ADIEU to Myself, star that day cannot efface!—sun locked in its meridian!—riderless courser through incomprehensible firmaments!

Adieu to Myself, marvellous Secret folded in the gray and amber coils of an innominate Dream!

BLACK SUNS
(1936)

The Overlord

Older than the wrinkles on the brow
Of Satan,
Younger than his smile,
My name is Liar,
And I dominate the worlds.

My brain is Space,
And those stars which run their race
To lying zeniths
Are my thoughts,
Red and nacre,
Green and yellow—
Thoughts that beckon gods and mortals
And all things blown from my fecund tongue,

My name is Liar,
And each day you may behold me
A-straddle the Sun,
The great Peacock of the Air,
And watch me ride to the high-noon of Hope
And slink down the western sky
To the music of your curses.

When the Sea of the Mind gives up its dead
I alone shall tread that Final Strand—
Older than the wrinkles on the brow
Of Satan,
Younger than his smile—
I alone,
Pierrot-Paraclete,
Munchausen of the Mocking Millenniums.

WALTER

Eyes,
Two wistful beams
From a sea-drowned moon—
Lips,
Two quivering, murderous blades—
Feet,
That hastened on toward
A Mecca in the stars.

O blown Rose!
O magic Jar!
Where are thy scents and all thy petals now?

The Decoy

Tomorrow,
That immortal jester,
Patched in the motley of our hopes,
Whose smile is as soft as a summer wind
In equatorial gardens,
Whose tread is lighter than the footfall of ghosts—
Leads us with a beck in his eye
And a painted bauble in his hand
Into the presence of his Lord Death,
Who with a gesture of an eyelash
Prorogues our parleys with Circumstance
And inters us with our memories and hopes,
Still fat upon our wills,
In the sealed dungeons of
Oblivion.

The Haunted House

My brain is a tropical forest,
Dark and sinister,
In whose branches thoughts dart and play
Like crimson scarabees—
A sea of phosphorescent light
In which images sport like flying fish.
A garden, too,
Wherein walk sadic Christs
And Neros that are Paraclete—
A seraglio peopled with scarlet angels
Who chant their hymns of passion
To the cataleptic Sultan of the Skies.

My brain is a chariot of sun-motes
Drawn by two great butterflies
Caught by Moon-Titans,
Who carry me past the sparkling sweat-beads
On the face of the celestial Ethiope
And the multi-billioned infusoria
Who pullulate in their depths
To the solemn solitudes of the Nirvana of fairies
Who drowse forever on the Golden Thigh of Pythagoras.

My brain! My brain!
A star exiled from Space
To the Siberia of my skull
Without reprieve!

Marche Funebre

Sadness,
Beautiful as a girl who wanders
Into the dark waters of the night,
Lifts its flooded eyes toward this hour,
Impregnate with silence and memories,
And the Minutes pass before my ear
Like tocsins sounded on leaden cymbals.

CHIMERAS

Chimeras of melancholy Mount from my brain—
My brain, an ancient-ruined sun
With jets of fire still spurting through a cleft—
Mount beyond the mangled magnificences of crumbled pasts
And the caesarism of the dead.

Red chimeras,
Green chimeras,
Chimeras that were once choral Ariels
That sang in the rigging of my brain.

Chimeras! Chimeras!

Chimeras of melancholy
Mount from my brain—
My brain, a lost Pacific of a thousand tropic isles,
Gleaming like sea-begotten Pleiades—
Mount beyond the summits of my will
And the ice-locked gargoyles of the moon.

Red chimeras,
Green chimeras,
Chimeras that rally like furloughed memories
At the trumpet-call of Death.

Chimeras! Chimeras!

Magical Night

My withered dreams rebloomed last night,
And to the strains of a triumphal march
Played on the keys of the hours
By the Blind Beethoven of the Stars
I wandered again
With Lilith and Eve and Cain and Orpheus
Through the elf-haunted gardens of my youth.

Fantasia

A monstrous black Eunuch
With a breech-clout of stars
Rose out of the Abyss.
In his right hand he held an
Open red parasol,
Which were the mathematical points
Of the spaces above him.
On the middle finger of his left hand,
Outstretched before,
Gleamed a ring of bleeding rubies.
And as he walked toward the ecliptic
Of the Earth
I heard a rumor in my soul:
"Behold him!—
The Final Absurdity,
The impotent incarnation of the
Fantasy of Life!"

In the Backyard of Life

My dreams,
Like withered flowers,
Hang on the crumpled stalk of my will,
And the chill wind of an immortal disgust
Blows the pollen of my hopes
Against the privies of Reality.

Man

I am Man,
Star-gymnast,
Buffoon to the Fatal Presence,
Wearing the motley of Change,
A stale platitude in the mouth of a Wit.

I am Man,
The comic almanac of God,
Now gangrened with routine,
Now melting away at Waterloo and Verdun
In the rays of Its invisible purpose.

I am Man—
The Christ and the Buddha,
Napoleon and Shelley, Aurelius and Attila;
In my eye the beat of celestial thunders,
In my Heaven but one star—
Pride.

I am Man—
Stark from the Mystery,
Strapped in the scarlet Chariot of Hope
That rolls over the suns;
About my head beat the livid lightnings
Of sudden apprehensions.

I am Man—
Prometheus-Cagliostro,
With the bloody thumb-print of Medusa
On my whitest thought;
An exile in my own skull,
Suburb of Death.

I am Man—
Fire that thinks and feels,
Dust of a thousand planets,
A remorse in the brain of God!

Shelley

Clothed in a star,
A rainbow for a girdle,
His solar hair floated over the horizons of worlds.
Taller than Thor,
Mutinous as Prometheus,
His steps wove Utopias
As he flashed toward Lyra,
Cleaving seas of ether in his flight,
The glory of his eyes
Firing the Cosmos with a newer splendor.

Imagination

I am Imagination,
Gorgeous rug that covers
The rotten floor of Reality—
A haunted chateau,
The red Pantheon of Lucifer,
Vestibule between Time and Eternity.

I am Imagination,
The North Star of Science,
The flambeau of the lover,
The whirling nebulae of the Poet,
The plasma of gods—
Puck strapped to the back of Rosinante,
Fire-runged ladder to the Fourth Dimension.

I am Imagination,
The seignory of untrammelled instincts,
A fief of unsanctified dreams—
Shakespeare to the Soul,
Golden key to the Bastilles of Logic,
A sublime and beatified liar
Demiurge of Myth and Hope.

Keats

Avatar of the Bitter Beauty,
Paramour to Aphrodite and Helena,
At the bazaars of Life-and-Death,
The soul of John Keats
Was a migratory Chimera
Whose vast diaphanous wings were caught and broken
In the Tree of Good and Evil.

Facts

To follow the May winds to
The limbo of dead winters;
To climb the rungs of the tempest
'Till I reach the Cave of the Thunders
And the Smithy of Lightnings;
To perch on the brim of a wester-going cloud
Till it dissolve in the Sea of Japan;
Or to curve, worm-wise, in the ear of Echo,
Listening in on the slaughters for the Ideal
On the Astral Plane—
      These are *my* Facts!

To be the bezel of a star;
Aura of fairies
That play on the crests of candle flames;
Breath of Boreas
As he moulds monumental bergs
For gullible Titanics;
Or the mirror of the Infinite
That is a baby's eye—
      These are *my* Facts!

To be 'prisoned in a snowflake
As it melts on the lips of my love;
To be that insane god
Who begat the Earth on the body of the Sun;
To be the measured movement of light
As it swims to evasive zeniths;
Or witches that feed on St. Elmo fires
That circle over the graves of poets—
      These are *my* Facts!

Strange, ephemeral races that live in sand-bubbles;
The ghosts of material things latent in chimney-smoke;
The pixies that burrow in the pebbled depths of fountains;
Inter-atomic beings who bathe forever in the magic rays

Struck from their drowsy dreams—
    These are *my* Facts!

To make a gorgeous noose of Saturn's rings
Wherewith to hang myself;
To mount the Hippogrif
As it hurtles toward chimeric planets;
To dance with Puck
Upon the dusty skull of human Reason—
    These are *my* Facts!

Facts! O world,
Muzzy with reason and rules!
There is only one Fact:
The Gemmèd Brain of the Poet—
That magic bubble of Maya
Blown from her lying, voluptuous lips!

The Tragic Bluffer

I saw Martial Courage
Fleeing in the night
When the stars slept
And the sentinel Pride lay huddled in dreams—
Saw him fleeing toward his home
In the bosom of Cowardice,
Fleeing the gray eye of
Irony,
That threw in its wake its enormous
Grin.

The Humorist

I am Hope,
Venomous satirist
With the eye of a babe;
Iago
Playing a guitar beneath the windows of
Grief;
Giant flambeau in the hand of
Satan
That lights the Race down the ages to the
Perpetual Festal Worm.

I am Hope,
Immaculate conception of the virgin womb
Credulity;
Brazen Valkyrie of the spirit
Who carries the corpses of her Siegfrieds
To the Pantheons of ice in
Oblivion.

I am Hope,
Fairy godmother of Despair;
Flying feet of Dawn
That you pursue down the ridges of an eternal
Night;
A toy balloon escaped from the hand of a child
Which collapses on the frozen mountains of the
Moon.

Dawn

Day the fratricide
Hath murdered his brother Night
And hid his body in the western sky.
Triumphant Titan,
He stands upon the eastern mountain tops
Bathed in foaming blood,
And in his forehead sparkles Lucifer,
The morning star.

Sleep

I am Sleep,
Gray nimb of Death,
Impresario of hushed spectacles,
Sculptor of trans-earthly colossi
That I work with thumb and forefinger
In the plasm of your brain.

Now I woo you to the infoliate depth
Of my utter shadow,
And you who are chin-deep in time
And brain-deep in eternity
Float at the bottom of a waveless sea
Toward vortices of silence.

The pomp of Prospero
And the necromancy of Cagliostro
That you called your world,
And the noiseless ghosts
That parley in your arteries
That you called your Self
Are immigrant,
With all their tinsel and blab, to my
Nullibeity.

I am Sleep,
The shoreless ocean,
Sinister aquarium of the Dead.

The Pickpocket

In the Street of the Years
I prowl, in the light, in the dark,
An immortal phantom
Mailed in impenetrable veils.
I pick stars out of the pockets of Space,
And from the pockets of your skull
I deftly lift all your dreams
And pile them sky-high—
Stars and dreams—
In the backyard of the Past—
For I am Time,
The pickpocket,
Shoplifter to His Majesty.

Vers Libre

I am the formless form,
The line of least resistance,
The anarch and dissolver of style.
I am raw, primitive,
A bridge between harmony
And a newer and greater diapason.

I am a Beethoven of Dissonance,
The Paderewski of the calliope,
A Paganini who saws out music
On giant cables of catgut—
A grotesque democratic skyscraper
Built of stones from the Parthenon,
Towers from the Kremlin,
Cornices and ruined balustrades from the Alhambra
And gables from a Mansion in the Skies,
All slammed together
Whimsically, carelessly.

For I am *Vers Libre*,
The careless god;
As careless as Nature, dreams and children,
Who have neither rhyme nor reason,
And wot not—
As careless as Life,
Which has neither beginning nor end,
Nor metre, nor beat,
Whose cadences,
Like mine,
Begin Nowhere and
Go Nowhither.

Immanent,
I existed before mind or the beat of feet
Was born
In a state of flux,

Nebulous,
Fourth-dimensional,
Protean,
Infoliate—
A Thought without words,
A Tongue that stammered out suns.

But I have a rhythm all my own,
Latent in the
Unarithmetical smile of Aeschylus,
Incarnate in the
Cosmoramic visions of Blake,
Strophied in the brains of the
Magis of Apprehension,
Who dream in the
Whirlwinds of Chaos.

I have the rhythm of the
God of Spinoza
And the sweep of his giant Modalities,
And my beat is the battle-beat of
Ormuzd and Ahriman.
I am the poesy of the Thing-in-Itself,
Unrelated,
A-shimmer with Wonder.

I am *Vers Libre*,
The Soul of Man,
That beats with the
Unknown
And that rhymes with the
Eternal X.

A Son of God

I carry the frightful stellar spaces in my brain
And see between my Will and the blazing stars of Hope
Such ineluctable spaces
That were my soul an eagle
Dressed in wings from lightnings made,
Its million-centuried flight
Would leave it farther from those radiant gleams
Than the Sphinx
Squat motionless in the sand.

The Ideal

The hoof of my Thought
Paws at the cobbles of Reality
While its scarlet wings unfold
In the pounding winds of treacherous summits
And its eyes open wide
At the sting of the stars.

Away! Away!
Beyond the fiery ramparts of new-born suns,
Beyond the frozen eyes of moons but newly-dead,
The hoof of my Thought
Thunders on the crests of trans-stellar cyclones—
As I ride toward the snowy solitudes
Of my private Mecca,
Luminous, ironic Mirage of Space!

Miracles

The subtle metamorphosis of lines
That sculpt Chimborazo out of sea-mud,
The veiled transmigrations of the dead,
Who re-beget themselves in their own graves;
The mysterious drama of circles
That we call History;
Karma, that guides the amoeba to the brain of Shakespeare
And that routes the way of the ant to the skull of Napoleon—
These are the obvious miracles
That no Water-Walker can explain.

Sea-Mania

Sea that whistles and sea that sobs,
Sea of the shadowy masks of death,
Sea of the dancing spiral beams,
    Sea of the blusterful mouth—
    Nacre and gray
    Like a bulgy snake,
    Sown with dimples
    Like a baby's chin—
O alkahest of the stony earth, fantastic chemist of steel and flesh,
    Receive me!

Sea that rants and sea that coos,
Sea of the thousand horizons,
Sea of the hoarse Valkyrean calls,
    Sea of the corpse-shod feet—
    Mansions of coral
    Awaiting your guests,
    Beds of flowers
    Awaiting drowned lovers—
O vagabond with the shoulder-shrug at the business of the suns,
    Receive me!

Sea of the gray-blue iron jaws,
Sea of the syncopated breath,
Sea of the light-blown ecstasies,
Sea of the vast ironic smile—
    Saliva of Neptune
    Blown 'gainst the stars,
    Playground of Sappho,
    Chasing discorporate moons—
O mausoleum with the roof of suns and floor of staring eyes,
    Receive me!

Strayling

A tiny hair on my overcoat
Coming whence I know not,
Trembling and wavering in the light winds,
Desiring to go—
Like the wandering hair that I am,
Blown 'gainst the grey mantle of Life,
Trembling and wavering in the strong winds
Of passion,
Desiring to go,
To go.

Ave, Zarathustra!

The Dancer on the Crumbling Edge
Weaves his way from Ledge to Ledge.
He dares the things we do not dare,
He mocks abyss, he treads the air
He makes of Fate a dazzling stair.
His feet are light, his lilt is gay,
From Crest to Crest he wheels his way.
He dares the things we do not dare,
He mocks abyss, he treads the air,
He makes of Fate a dazzling stair—
Because to Conscience he gives no pledge,
This Dancer on the Crumbling Edge!

The Thief

Sudden ray in the East
Like the flash from a dark-lantern,
And Day, the crook, is born
As Night with all her treasures of love and wine
Flees before his assassinate eye and feline step.

SWINBURNE

Words
That were like melodious lutes at the lips of his soul,
Unremembered of the Earth,
Are printed in the Book of Elohim
And are read by epiphanous beings
In unmaterial spaces.

The Vat

I think the Universe
A vat,
A stupendous fermentation of
Suns and gnats and Shakespeares,
A stinking brew of joys and sorrows,
The juice of clotted wounds,
The acid of vengeful dreams
And the frozen nightmares of the dead—
That one day will be quaffed in a single draught
By a tired god
Who seeks a brand-new cocktail.

Masque of the Minutes

Minutes
Monumental, immemorial Minutes!
Shining oases and flying mirages
Across the sand-wastes of Time!
Fragile, immortal ephemeridae!
Writhing prisoners of Form!
Unkempt, murderous Minutes,
Marmoreal, hallucinating Minutes!
This is Walpurgis Night and Easter Morn,
And you shall unveil your selves to me!

A Pilgrim Minute
I am a Pilgrim Minute,
The Wandering Jew of Time,
And through all your incarnations
I have tiptoed down the corridors of your brains,
Lighted candle in hand,
Looking for God.

A Frozen Minute
I am Reason,
The winter of the emotions.
Webbed in algebraic formulas,
Cadenced in syllogisms,
Over Man I have no power,
For I have no soul.

A Desolate Minute
I was once a fly
In the Empyrean,
And I walked on the ceiling of the Universe
Flywise
And glanced into the Forbidden City
Of the Future.
Since then I am
The Niobe of Minutes.

A Black Minute
I am *Ennui*,
The frightful gargoyle
That completes the Temple of the Hours,
Creator and destroyer of worlds,
The black snowflake.

A Brazen Minute
I am Curiosity,
The assassin,
Traveller to Arcturus,
Tempter of virgins,
The brazen eye in the brain,
A Columbus of Ultima Thules.

A Gray Minute
I am Fatigue,
An eagle that yawns
In the face of the Infinite.
Space is a chicken-coop
And the stars are stud-farms.
I am weary of flight,
And my eyes are worn blind
With the dazzle and tinsel
Of inutile suns.
Once anarch of the skies,
My head now seeks the soft bolster of
Death.

An Ironic Minute
I am the last minute that lived
In the brain of
Christ.
And I heard him say this:
"I had not wisdom until Judas kissed me."
And he smiled and died.

A Murderous Minute
I am the brigand
Ridicule,
An antique Wasp,
The serious Harlequin,
An abettor of sanity—
The wisdom of the last man.

An Arcless Minute
I am the Will-to-Immobility,
Center of all circumferences,
Frozen magnet toward which dart
All that lives and all that dreams—
Infinite Comprehension
Swarming with nebulous and transcendent
Entities.
I am the Miraculous Minute of
Plotinus.

A Mystic Minute
I am a diver
Foraging in the sunken galleons
Of imponderable seas,
Sun-rifler and ether-walker—
A lizard, too,
That lies motionless on the walls of
Eternity.
I was the fulcrum-minute in the brain of
Blake,
And through me he lifted the
Stars.

A Nameless Minute
The brain is a carcass
Swarming with the vermin of thought,
A cemetery in which lie
A thousand ruined saviors
And a thousand rotting conquerors—

The blasphemous flower
Abloom on the grave of God.
I am the final minute in the brain of
Nietzsche.

AN ANARCH MINUTE
I hung upon the granite walls of the
Caucasus
And soared as a Curse
Out of the mouth of
Prometheus
Into the brain of
Jupiter.

AN ETERNAL MINUTE
Like a giant glow-worm,
I appeared at the zenith of the Night
And stabbed the dark with my flame,
Dying of my own light.
I was the minute called
Shelley.

A PASSIONATE MINUTE
The veil of the senses
Lay furled around my Thought
For a thousand years—
A thousand years the Thought
Stood mute and muffled
In its esoteric majesty.
Then away! away! we rode like a furious
Valkyrie
Toward an extinct Valhalla.
I was the crowning minute in the brain of the
Shadow-Eater.

A SPECTRAL MINUTE
I crossed the threshold of the
Ineluctable.

You cannot see me,
You must not know me.
I am the Ghastly One,
A minute in the brain of
Edgar Poe,
A prolonged note in the consciousness of
Chopin.
I whisper once to every one
Across the border of the Forbidden.
You cannot see me,
You must not know me—
I am the Beauty that blasts.

A Narcotic Minute
I am the bloodshot eye
Of sleepless Hope—
Hope,
The insomnia of Death.

A Twin-Born Minute
I am Beauty-and-Death,
Light and shadow of the Absolute.
When Lucifer was cast into Darkness
His brain became a sun—
Of that star am I twin-born.

A Hypocrite Minute
I am the triumphant Archangel
Of Universal Laughter,
The logic of survival,
The first and last Theocrat and Democrat.
My hostel is the Ideal—
My mirror is
Man.

A Cowled Minute
At the feast of the Furies
The human heart is the *pièce de résistance*—
Therefore am I the
Tear that floods the world,
Avatar of immedicable griefs,
The almanac of the dead.

A Philosophic Minute
Pale,
Thought-inwrapt,
Ears a-prick,
Upright at the heart of Chaos,
I heard the reverberations
Of thoughts unborn
As they thundered through skulls unconceived.
In the ancient Earth-nebula
I was Pythagoras and Nietzsche

A Static Minute
I am a Static Minute,
A mirror that no breath can mist.
Behind the swirl of moods
I glow, a full moon,
Perpetuate, untroubled.
I may be veiled,
But not obliterated—
For I am the Spectator of Change.

A Super-Minute
Death can waive me,
For in my soul I carry a private oblivion.
I apprehend and lapse;
I am the everlasting To-Be,
The Hegelian Becoming,
Imperishable Tantalus-Proteus,
The lethean years that flow
Into the hollow aeons of
Eternity.

THE FINAL MINUTE
Final Minute,
I dream of the mystery of Time—Time,
The Ararat of Eternity,
On whose summit is stranded
The Ark of Consciousness
For a little while—
For a little while!

Salutation

Let fall the glory on his head,
This poet, dead!
Let fall the laurel on his brow
Who is not now!

Let trumpets blow 'gainst sunlit skies
And ope his eyes!
Let rainbows glisten and dispart
And fuse his heart!

Let God awake and strike the Moon
From its icy swoon!
Let mage and sibyl come to his bed.
A poet's dead! A poet's dead!

INGRESSION

And now it is come time to die
And be solved again in the immurmurous ebb and flow
Of the omnipresent Breath.

With rapt expectancy that enkindles all my brain
And the mighty pantheistic thrill shot through my heart,
I await the revelations of change and the new Apocalypse
That lies beyond these soon obliterated senses—
Knowing with a faith that makes of creeds a blasphemous
    atheism
That in the laboratories of Pan no force is quenched
And that the atoms of my body are as necessary to the
    panharmonic sweeps of Life
As are my dreams in the psychoramas of Chance.

The cyclones of thought are freezing in my eye
And on my lips is graven the final scorn of Time and its partner,
    Corruption.
The hulk of my Dream is beating itself slowly to ruin
On the reef of conjecture,
And soon I shall be translated to that abstruse common place
That man calls "dust"—
Or be the beady drip of moonlight from the spired spurs of
    Andean peaks,
Or flying light-pollen of lost zodiacs
Or livid flame in a meteor that flees the ruin of some rotted
    constellation.
In the legions of some amazing Titan shall I be a soldier battling
    on an invisible star
Against some shadowy Zeus
After this little respite from splendid errors and absurd
    certainties
And the electric mystery of living?

O dumb, transcendental, elemental Spirit that wovest the stars
And the inverted infinities of the atom,

O thou who in thy blank and eyeless movement hast invented
The infoliate universe in the brain of the ant
And set within our blood the polyglot colloquies of the dead,
And didst sculpt the oceanic laugh in the skull of Rabelais;
O magical, ubiquitous Presence
Out of whose circumference I cannot step,
Beyond whose being nothing is:
O thou work-a-day One
Who sweatest suns and lightnings and Shakespeares, Bluebells
    and Caesars
And those countless shadows that talk and procreate and weep
    and go:
O thou Weaver that didst spin this skull around my brain
And didst weave these curtains for my tired eyes,
Thy will be done! Undo thy doing!

UNCOLLECTED, VARIATIONS, & TRANSLATIONS
(1897–1945)

Sorrow's Balm

When grief upon my spirit lies
    And o'er my eyes there comes a mist,
When day is filled with heated sighs
    And to the Giant's voice I list,

'Tis then I hear from far away
    A Voice attuned to human tears,
And with the gentleness of May
    It bids begone the phantom fears.

That Voice! That Voice! 'tis Hope, 'tis Rest,
    It lures my soul to brighter fields,
Where, in the Gardens of the Blest,
    To music sweet my sorrow yields.

---

* *The New Era-Lancaster*, July 31, 1897.

The Wisdom of Gautama

In the realm of the soul dwell the blessings of life;
Then desire is felt not, nor torment, and strife.
The prom thy soul craves is there to be found,
There the treasuries of life are with diadems crowned,
There are our loved ones who long since are dead,
And there the sweet dreams on which our youth fed.
The things that are tangible are not always real;
The prizes of life to the senses appeal;
The marmoreal beauty of dreams cannot fade,
Nor can wither the images by the soul made—
Thy soul will achieve without labor or tears
What thy flesh vainly chases through long phantom years.

* *The Evening Kansan-Republican*, Aug 30, 1898.

Prayer

All rational pleasure is prayer; all sincere work and effort are prayers; all exaltation in the presence of beauty is prayer; all aspiration is prayer.

Prayer is an uplifting, a rising of the soul toward the object of its desire, an elevation of instinct.

All sincere thought is prayer. The doubts of skeptics are prayers, though they themselves would repudiate the term.

All strength that tends to elevate and glorify man is a prayer.

There are other modes of praying than with the lips. Galileo prayed with a telescope. Columbus prayed with a ship. Franklin prayed with a lightning-rod.

Knee praying seems a puny thing when once we feel that the forests are the eternal fanes of nature; or when we stand on a mountain top, that everlasting natural altar; or when we bathe in sunlight, that incalculably aged censer.

Amid these natural objects awe, admiration, a sense of infinite force, of infinite life, of a duration that is eternal sweep through us in waves, leaving its humiliated with the sense of our own nothingness at the same time that it brings something of intellectual pride that we are part of that Hidden God.

All sublime emotion is prayer. A poem, a painting, a great essay, a beautiful face, the wreathing of a vine around a window, all exalt, generating a wonder, amazement, and thankfulness.

Meanness, lying, cowardice, double-dealing, these are all blasphemies; they offend the dignity of the soul, and debase you in your own eyes. The blasphemies of the mouth are laughed away in the winds. They mean nothing. But the blasphemies of vile actions set in motion forces that must be combated through all time.

Man prays when he least knows it. The normal evolution of prayer is from the lip to the deed, from bare utterance to strong action.

* *Cosmopolitan Magazine*, October, 1907.

Solitude

Friends, come sit beside me that I may feel the mighty distance between us.
Woman that I bind around in thongs of passion, what ghastly gulf is that between thy heart and mine!
I walk where men walk and sit where men sit and between me and them there lies the Infinite.
Behind the inscrutable aura of personality I reign a King, a Caesar throned in a Sahara.

* *The Papyrus*, October 1911.

Solitude

Amis, venez vous asseoir autour de moi que je puisse me rendre compte de l'énorme distance qui nous sépare.
O femme que j'enlace dans mes accès de passion, quel horrible abîme entre ton cœur et le mien.
Je me lève quand les autres hommes se lèvent, je me rasseois quand ils reprennent place, et entre eux et moi... intervient l'Infini.
Derrière l'inscrutable atmosphère de la personnalité, je règne tel un roi, tel un César au milieu d'un Sahara.

---

* *Hors du troupeau*, January–February 1912. Translated by E. Armand.

West Point

Gray and white automatons in the summer sunshine, wheeling, counter-wheeling in lockstep.
Above, in the wells of azure, crows wheeling and counter-wheeling in locked measures,
Their prophetic nostrils sensing the fields of slaughter still nebulous dreams in the brains of the
Gray and white automatons who wheel and counter-wheel in the glare of the summer sun.

* *The International*, February 1915.

Revelation

      Days when Nothing happens,
When the life in the brain and the heart seems shrivelled and
    dried up like a November leaf,
And our Will stares at us like the eye of a dead fish,
And we grasp the meaning of Nothing.

      Days when Nothing happens,
When the lips of Curiosity are bloodless and anathema marantha
    is pronounced 'gainst all Art,
And the eyes of our love are the eyes of a Jezebel
And we grasp the meaning of the Nothing.

---

* *The International*, February 1915.

Late Autumn

Falling leaves sighing like dying fairies,
Frou-frou of death on the forest breeze,
A white flake in the air whirled from world-end,
    The winter is coming, coming tiptoe.

---

* *The International*, February 1915.

An Incident

Builded of prisms, old gold and green, the Temple of Paphos rose
 in the depths of the wine,
Liszt's lecherous Second came to me from the Tzgaines behind
 the palms
The while I felt her hand, white and cold, sweep my cheek,
And on her breath there was the humid warmth of unwindowed
 sepulchres—
 The Feast was at an end.

I rolled a crum of bread between my thumb and index like God
 contours a planet,
And with my other hand I plunged a dagger in her heart
And cancelled in a tidal wave of red the Paphian Temple of
 prismatic gold and green—
 The Feast was at an end.

* *The International*, February 1915.

In the Slums

Downtown, in the poorer quarters of my soul, in the slums of myself, I saw and heard this thing:
A high old Spanish doorway, like the doorway of a Prison, left half open by Some One.
On an old chair with three legs, in the middle of the Room, sat an Old Man, wrapped in a blanket, his head half-bowed as though in a doze.
There is a scamper of Rats near him; and he does not move.
There is a long, loud wail from Somewhere Within, a squalid wail, a wail weird and sharp that pierces the Air and reaches the brilliantly lighted avenues of my Consciousness.
But there is never a stir from the drowsing Figure on the three-legged chair-throne of repentance!
It all happened down there in the poorer quarters of myself, in the slums of my soul, far from the brilliantly lighted avenues of my Consciousness.

* *The International*, February 1915.

My Lamp

The twilight blots out the sunbeams one by one on the wall above
    my lamp,
And in their place come three giant moths with amber wings.
Immobile, they watch for the golden glimmer from the light.
To open their amber wings and to feel the thrill of death.

---

* *The International*, February 1915.

Bio

I, a soldier of dreams, came to the fortress of my Ideal,
She was deliriously dark, and high on the ramparts of her body were set two great casements flaming with a strange fire.
She looked at me from out of her twin casements and made signals as if to a banquet spread in the Jasper Halls of her Heart.
There was a deep moat between us then, and I could not cross to the magic gate of her being swinging open for the soldier of dreams—the lord of the Jasper Halls of her Heart.
She, divine Amazon of Love, waits there for me now that I have returned from my son in Hell, the moat is paved over with onyx and gold, and I clamber wildly up the sweet rampart of her being and enter the Jasper Halls of her Heart.
There are flutes and fountains and rare vintages for the Hunter and his Faithful One, tears and sobs and the fairy stories of Two Hearts whispered to the sound of flutes and fountains and wild-throated nightingales.

* *The International*, February 1915.

The Gallic Lark and the Sow-on-the Rhine

—To France in arms.

THE LARK (*whirling in the azure*):
    I orbit in the suns of my Vision, my heart is the Grail of Life.
    I am France, the Athens of Europe, Dionysiac, singing in strife.
THE SOW-ON-THE-RHINE:
    I am the mother of nations, I am the savior of men,
    I am the Sphinx and Revealer—thou art but a winged hen.
THE LARK:
    I sing the Song of the Ages, I sing the song of the free,
    I sang in the heart of Ronsard, and the Voice in the Maid
        was of me!
THE SOW-ON-THE-RHINE:
    Give me your wings and your lightness, give me your dreams
        and your Eye—
    I hate thee, I love thee, thou wild bird—come down and live
        in my sty.
THE LARK:
    O Sow that would be Alborak! O Sow of Elysian dreams!
    Thy sty is the dung-pit of learning, they snout with Flemish
        blood gleams.
THE SOW-ON-THE-RHINE:
    Curse thy lilt and thy wild heart, curse the air and the light
        thou dost cleave!
    Curse the Song thou dost sing to thy Loved Ones, who of
        thy songs Victory weave!
THE LARK:
    I orbit in the suns of my Vision, my heart is a Grail and an Inn;
    My songs have annealed into iron, old Sow with the helmet
        of tin!

---

* The first example of this poem is a postcard, published around early-to-mid 1915. It was later reprinted in the *New-York Tribune*, April 23, 1918.

L'Alouette Gauloise et la Truie du Rhin

À la France en armes.

L'Alouette tournoyant dans l'azur:
>Je tourne dans les soleils de ma vision, mon cœur est le clairon de la vie.
>Je suis la France, l'Athènes de l'Europe, je suis dionisiaque, je chante dans la bataille.

La Truie:
>Je suis la mère des nations, je suis le salut des hommes, je suis le sphinx et le révélateur—et toi tu n'es qu'une poule blessée.

L'Alouette:
>Je chante le chant des siècles, je chante le chant de la liberté
>Je chantais dans le cœur de Ronsard, la voix de la Vierge était ma voix.

La Truie:
>Donne-moi tes ailes et ta légèreté, donne-moi tes songes et ton œil.
>Je te hais, je t'aime, oiseau sauvage, descends et viens dans mon étable.

L'Alouette:
>Ô truie qui te voudrais divine! Ô truie aux rêves élyséens, ton étable est le trou à fumier de la science et ton museau est tout rouge de sang.

La Truie:
>Maudite sois-tu, toi et ton cœur sauvage, maudit soit l'air où tu planes!
>Maudit le chant que tu chantes pour tes bien-aimés, le chant dont ils tissent leur victoire.

L'Alouette:
>Je tourne dans les soleils de ma vision, mon cœur est un clairon, mes chants forgent le fer, ô vieille truie, au casque d'étain!

---

* *Dans la tourmente*, April–July, 1915. A translation by Rémy de Gourmont of "The Gallic Lark and the Sow-on-the Rhine".

Pater Noster

Où es-tu, ô Dieu? Viens et sois jugé, sois frappé, sois exécuté par moi.
Où es-tu, ô Dieu? Être subtil, être rusé, constructeur du Ciel et de l'Enfer, amant de l'Esprit et de la Matière, viens et sois jugé, sois frappé, sois exécuté par moi.
J'ai croisé à ta recherche jusqu'à cette heure à travers l'éternité. Viens et sois jugé, sois frappé, sois exécuté par moi.

Maintenant, en voilà assez, mangeur d'hommes, multiforme cannibale, molécule de l'assassinant, Thug dans la nuit.
N'y a-t-il pas assez de sang sur ton autel, n'y a-t-il pas assez de chair sur ta table, n'y a-t-il pas assez de puanteur sous tes narines?
Maintenant il faut que cela finisse, poltron, fuyard, Borgia de l'Éternité, Iago de l'éther.

Anti-Dieu, je suis; et je suis sur le toit de ton tabernacle mystique comme un voleur dans la nuit.
Anti-Dieu, je suis; et je suis sur le seuil de ton secret comme une vengeresse Érynnie.
Anti-Dieu, je suis; et je suis la langue des victimes de ta loi de Nécessité dont les gouttes de sang jonchèrent le monde pendant cette dernière année de ton règne.

Je te jette à la face les seins et les ovaires des femmes découpées par les mains de tes créatures.
Je te jette à la face une énorme poignardée de testicules et de phallus arrachés par les mains de tes créatures.
Je te jette à la face les corps rôtis de petits enfants jetés au feu par les mains de tes créatures.

Auteur de la Vie et auteur de la Mort, écoute, oh! écoute le tonnerre de ma haine!

* *Mercure de France*, May 1, 1915. Translated by Remy de Gourmont.

Auteur de la Vie et Auteur de la Mort, écoute, oh! écoute la prodigieuse malédiction que je prononce sur toutes tes œuvres.
Auteur de la Vie et Auteur de la Mort, écoute, oh! écoute l'appel passionné de celui qui ne peut être trompé, qui ne peut être réduit au silence, qui ne peut être enchaîné par tes menaces.

Anathema maranatha sur ton éblouissant Cosmos, masque de ton perpétuel diabolisme! Amen.
Anathema maranatha sur les jours de printemps et sur ceux de l'été, sur l'automne et sur les neiges de l'hiver, masques de ton perpétuel diabolisme! Amen.
Anathema maranatha sur la race humaine, outil de ton perpétuel diabolisme! Amen.

Maudite soit la Vie, cette stupide aventure!
Maudit soit le coït, ce stupide plaisir!
Maudite soit l'épée, cette stupide peine!

Tu as créé l'homme à ton image, et tu lui as donné un toit à porcs pour maison.
Tu as créé l'homme à ton image, et tu lui as donné la guerre pour apprentissage.
Tu as créé l'homme à ton image et tu lui as donné pour vin le sang de ses frères.

Apogée de notre amertume, apogée de notre martyre, l'égout et le vomissement des cycles de la vie te montent jusqu'aux fesses, Torquemada des cieux, perpétuel Néron de l'éternité.
Cependant les cœurs sensibles ont le droit de redire en minaudant:
    Aux petits des oiseaux il donne la pâture
    Et sa bonté s'étend sur toute la nature.

Pater Noster

Unde eşti, o, D-zeule? Vino, să fii judecat, isbit, executat de mine.
Unde eşti, o, D-zeule? Fiinţă subtilă, fiinţă şireată, ziditor al cerului şi al Infernului, amant al Spiritului şi al Materiei vino să fii judecat, isbit, executat de mine.
Am cutreerat în căutarea ta eternitatea: vino să fii judecat, isbit, executat de mine.

Ţi-ajunge, mâncător de oameni, canibal multiform, moleculă a asasinatului, Thug al nopţii.
Nu-i de ajuns sânge pe altarul tău, carne la masa ta, duhoare sub nările tale?
Să sfârşească odată, poltron, Borgia al Eternităţii, Iago al Eterului!

Anti-D-zeu sunt; şi sunt sub acoperişul tabernaculului tău mistic, ca un tâlhar în noapte.
Anti-D-zeu sunt; şi sunt pe pragul Tainei tale ca o răzbunătoare Erynnie.
Anti-D-zeu sunt; şi sunt graiul victimelor legii tale, numită necesitatea, ale cărei şuvoaie de sânge năpădiră lumea în acest din urmă an al stăpânirii tale.

Îţi arunc în obraz sânii femeilor ciopârtite de mâna creaturilor tale.
Îţi arunc în obraz un pumn uriaş de organe smulse de mâna creaturilor tale.
Îţi arunc în obraz trupurile prăjite ale copilaşilor aruncaţi în flăcări de mâna creaturilor tale.

Plămăditor al Vieţii şi al Morţii, ascultă, o, ascultă urletul urii.
Plămăditor al Vieţii şi al Morţii ascultă, o, ascultă, năvalitoarea bârfire ce o rosteşte atrocea gură a operelor tale.
Plămăditor al Vieţii şi al Morţii, ascultă, o, ascultă, râsul pătimat

---

* *Flacăra literară, artistică, socială*, July 11, 1915. Translated by Constantin Banu.

al celui ce nu poate râde, nimic nu tace, întunericul tău
neantul urii!"

Anathema maranatha asupra orbitorului tău Cosmos, mască a
perpetuului tău diabolism. Amin.
Anathema maranatha asupra zilelor de primăvară și de vară,
asupra toamnei și zăpezilor de iarnă, măști ale perpetuului
tău diabolism. Amin.
Anathema maranatha asupra rasei umane, unealtă a
perpetuului tău diabolism. Amin.

Blestemată fie viața, această stupidă aventură.
Blestemată procreația, această stupidă plăcere.
Blestemată sabia, această stupidă cazna.

Ai creat pe om după chipul tău și i-ai dat o cotineață drept casă.
Ai creat pe om după chipul tău și i-ai dat războiul drept meserie.
Ai creat pe om după chipul tău și i-ai dat drept vis sângele fratelui
lui.

Apogeu al amărăciunilor noastre, apogeu al martiriului nostru,
haznaua ciclurilor vieții să ți se verse până la brâu,
    Torquemada al Cerurilor,
    Nero al Eternității!

Pater Noster

Where are you, O God? Come and face judgment, be struck down, and executed by me.
Where are you, O God? Subtle schemer, cunning architect, builder of Heaven and Hell, lover of Spirit and Matter—come and face judgment, be struck down, and executed by me.
I have wandered eternity in search of you—come and face judgment, be struck down, and executed by me.

Enough now, man-eater, shape-shifting cannibal, storm of slaughter, night stalker.
Is there not yet enough blood on your altar? Enough flesh upon your table? Enough stench beneath your nostrils?
Now it must end, coward, fugitive, Borgia of Eternity, Iago of the ether.

Anti-God, I am; and I stand on the roof of your mystical tabernacle like a thief in the night.
Anti-God, I am; and I stand at the threshold of your secret like an avenging Erinys
Anti-God, I am; and I am the tongue of the victims of your pitiless Law of Necessity, whose bloodied drops soaked the world in the last year of your reign.

I hurl in your face the breasts and ovaries of women torn apart by the hands of your creatures.
I hurl into your face a butchers mass of testicles and phalluses, torn by the hands of your creatures.
I hurl in your face the roasted bodies of little children thrown into the fire by the hands of your creatures.

Author of Life and Death, listen, oh! Hear the thunder of my hatred!
Author of Life and Death, listen, oh! Hear the colossal curse I

---

* A new English translation has been prepared for this volume.

pronounce over all your works.
Author of Life and Death, listen, oh! Hear the passionate cry of one who cannot be deceived, cannot be silenced, cannot be chained by your threats.

Anathema maranatha on your dazzling Cosmos, mask of your eternal devilry! Amen.
Anathema maranatha on the days of spring and those of summer, on autumn and the snows of winter, masks of your perpetual devilry! Amen.
Anathema maranatha on the human race, tool of your perpetual devilry! Amen.

Cursed is Life, that witless farce!
Cursed is Sex, that fool's delight!
Cursed is War, that brutish sorrow!

You created man in your image, and you gave him a pigsty for a home.
You created man in your image, and you gave him war as his apprenticeship.
You created man in your image, and you gave him his brothers' blood as wine.

At the height of our bitterness, at the height of our martyrdom, the sewage and vomit of the cycles of life rise to your very haunches, Torquemada of the skies, eternal Nero of the æons.

Yet tender hearts still lisp with pious airs:
He gives the smallest birds their nourishment,
And over all His works extends His goodness.

To Emile Verhaeren

Titan of Flanders, whose brain is a tocsin of gold and whose
    breath is the clamor of tempests,
Vulcan of the tears and the sobs of *Les Soirs* and the paens and
    shouts of *Les Forces Tumultueuses*,
Dionysiac avatar of the mystical-sensuous soul of old Belgium,
Forge in the flames of Aerschot and Louvain the Song of
    Vengeance and Victory.

Moulder of lightnings and thunders, architect of the crashing
    and withering thought.
Seest thou not on the roofs of Antwerp and Brussels the great
    scarlet buzzards, the winged colossi from over the Rhine?
Emile Verhaeren! Out from the Pantheon down by the Seine
    waters the voice of the Titan of *Les Châtiments* is calling—
Is calling to thee to forge in the flames of Aerschot and Louvain
    the Song of Vengeance and Victory!

---

* *The Sun*, November 21, 1915.

The Haunted House

My brain is like a tropical forest, dark and sinister,
In whose branches and hedges thoughts dart and play like scarlet scarabees;
Or, sometimes, like a sea of phosphorescent light
In which images sport like flying fish.

A garden, too, wherein walk sadic Christ, and Neros that are Paraclete,
Which on a sudden changes into a seraglio peopled with scarlet angels
Who choir their prayers of passion to a cataleptic Sultan.

In fortunate hours it is like a chariot made of sun-motes
Drawn by two great butterflies caught by Titans of the Moon,
And it carries me past the sparkling sweat-beads on the face of the celestial Ethiope
And the sorrows of the multi-billioned creatures who pullulate in their depths
To the solemn solitudes of the Nirvana of fairies who drowse forever on the Golden Thigh of Pythagoras.

My brain! my brain! 'Tis star-exiled from space
And sent to the Siberia of my skull without reprieve;
A stomach that I shall one day disembowel,
Whose spilling. shall become beautiful words and shall dance and dance away!

---

* *Others*, 1916. This is an earlier variant of the poem of the same title (pg. 162).

The Mysterious Weaver

Time the weaver of life,
Time the unraveller of death
Is busy a-weaving across the seas
A monstrous Rune
To the rhyme of a croon
That wells from the Londons of the dead.

* *The Sun,* January 16, 1916.

Potporri

The hossannahs of the nations ring against the air.
There is a tocsin ringing at the top of the world.
Pity has become a molten tear.
Listen to the clang-clang of the giant crematorium as it rolls over the battlefield!
See the pretty dirigible that is throwing iron kisses to the dreadnoughts dressed in gray!
See the pretty soldiers in two hundred mile array swallowing steel bonbons!
The world has locked its front door and thrown the key away.
The Jews in Russia are to have free matzohs.
There is a death-rattle in the throats of the Dominations and Principalities.
This the twilight of the Kings, for they wear the entrails of mankind for crowns.
(The Promethean spark flickers low in the breast of mankind.)
The Tetrarchs of Hell are doddering of God while the blood of man makes crimson rainbows against the emptied ether!
Man, the cat's paw of the ages!
Man, eternal Uriah to criminal King Davids!
Man, you are to have free matzohs from the Romanoffs and the God-be-wid-ye of Hohenzollern and Hapsburg!
Pro Patria! Vive la Mort!

* *Revolt,* January 29, 1916.

W.S.: 1616–1916

You are not buried where your body lies,
Where matter and the worms hold long carousel
But there, atop the catafalque of Night,
Where Aldebaran has beatified your soul with light,
You await the magic touch of the eternal Prospero.

---

* *The Sun*, February 13, 1916. Commemorating the 300th anniversary of William Shakespeare's death.

The Hague—1915

Musical, mystical Jew, prince of all dreamers, king of all poets, sweetest among men!
Prophets foreran thee, stars left their orbits to glitter over thy cradle, O mystical, musical Jew!
Thy name hangs over the world like a banner of light and they story, O mystical, musical Jew, is the epic of Time.
O mystical, musical Jew! pale progenitor of Torquemada, Kishinef and The Marne—HAIL!

* *Revolt*, February 5, 1916.

Night Cometh

Night cometh!
The twilight steps through the city—
There'll soon be a glut of stars in the west.
The dens of imagination will send forth their beasts,
And a myriad love-cells will catch their bolts of honey.
Night cometh!
The Intellect rebegins its hopeless siege of God;
The sanctified profit-whores fill the vaudeville loges;
The world grows strumpet-wise as the twilight seeps through the
    city,
And the Blackguard of the Skies begins his sinister watch from
    his star-crowned tower in the West.
Night cometh!

---

* *Revolt*, February 5, 1916.

Song of Songs

Jesus came and sang for me—
      Bitter was my night!
Jesus came and wept for me—
      Bitter was my night!

Satan came and sat with me—
      A harp sang in the night!
Satan came to play with me—
      A harp sang in the night!

---

*   *Revolt*, February 5, 1916.

The Humorist

And the Great Secret stood before me nude and said:
"I am called Hope,
Venomous satirist with the eye of a babe,
Iogo playing the dulcimer beneath the windows of Grief,
Giant flambeau in the hand of Satan that lights the Race down
    the ages to the perpetual Festal Worm.

"I am called Hope,
The trumpet-call to the Ambuscade,
Immaculate conception of the virgin womb Credulity,
Brazen Valkyrie of the Spirit who carries the corpses of the slain
    to the wintry palaces of the obliterated.

"I am called Hope,
The fairy godmother of Despair,
Flying feet of Dawn that you pursue down the ridges of the
    Night,
Scintillant larva of the livid stare, a toy balloon escaped from the
    hand of a child, which collapses on the frozen mountains of
    the Moon.
I am called Hope."

---

* *Life*, March 1916. This is a variant of the poem of the same title (pg. 175).

Birth of a Sword

Wavering, misty, uncertain, a Thought begins to agglomerate and
 sparkle on the eastern horizon of my brain,
Lifting with its mysterious power strange sea buried and air laden
 with streamers,
Monsterous, shimmering sea wrack and air wrack from the
 depths of me.

A moment of doubt, a groping in the clouds, like a blind Dream
 searching for an eye.
Then a sudden crystallisation, a furious swirl of sea wrack and air
 wrack around the blazing nebula,
And a giant shaft of light is shot from the heart of the Thought
 across mountain and moorland—
And an Epigram is born unto me this day!

* *Greensboro Daily News,* March 15, 1916 (stated "in New York Sun").

Across the Gulf

The smooth white bellies of sharks.
Thunder clouds on the horizon like giant murder masks.
Perfumes from the undiscovered isles foundered in immeasurable
    depths,
The eternal shambles of the spaces,
The perpetuate moan of the sea deep dead,
And our three brains from the captain's bridge laying siege to the
    fortified mysteries of God!

*   *The Sun*, March 26, 1916.

The Conquerors

The great Field Marshal of the German hosts lies deep in sleep
    under the wide-awake eye of Riga,
When, a-sudden, the ears of his immurmurous blood are a-prick
    to listen to a buzz from a far place,
And the eye of his far-plotting brain, now sealed and nothing-
    worth,
Rolls up its leaden eyelid to behold a giant psychorama that
    moves across and down the precipices of his brain.

Achilles, Menelaus, Agamemnon, in the struck silence of death,
Glide past eyeless, like eagles that have shattered their heads
    'gainst multitudinous suns,
Or like those lustreless sockets in skulls where festal battle-
    buzzards have been.
Hannibal, Scipio, Caesar, with the nooses of mortality still
    dangling from their fleshless necks,
Flee from their glory toward stars that recede into ironic
    infinities.

Attila, whose eyes are the ghost-walk of slaughtered races;
Genghis Khan, whose body sweats serpents and whose hair is the
    entrails of murdered babes,
Roll by in iron chariots whose wheels are a-glisten with blood
    and flattened hearts.
Their lips are parted in a livid leer as if to pronounce that
    tremendous Nada! of Goya.

And Napoleon comes, greatest of all the Captains of Blood, first-
    born among the Knights of Massacre.
There were decrees in the folds of his lips and a Star gnawed at his
    brain like a rat,
And Necessity, as tall as God, scourged his flesh to fiery zephyrs
    Which floated beyond the stars, those St. Helenas of Space.

* *Seven Seas Magazine*, May 1916. It was illustrated on the facing page with "Der Krieg" by Franz von Stuck.

Now a fanfare blown from clarions at the tired lips of dying colossi
On the walls of a Valhalla crumbling beneath the breath of Oblivion,
And the psychorama fades, and the Conquerors of the Earth fall into bits of nothing.

The great Field Marshal of the German hosts writhes and twists in his frozen delirium,
Feeling near his spirit the rummaging nose of death,
Having beheld the Mardi Gras of the Worm.

In the Ramble

The sun weaves its mystery of shadow in the forest
And the river flows, like my thought, pensive and serene.
A gray mist soon will strangle the shadows in the forest.
The day elves will disappear in their holes in the air.
And the river will fade from my sight like a sweet thought
    forgotten.

* *The Sun*, May 3, 1916.

Fifty!

Fifty to-day!
And suddenly I saw my years as a series of pyramidal gray heaps,
Tiny ashen mounds lying in the golden receiver of the Past.
What god has used my soul as a cigar?

* *The Kansas City Star,* June 11, 1916.

The Pacifist's Breviary

If a fire breaks out in your house speak to it gently.
The universe is a product of non-resisting forces.
Time enough to learn to swim when the boat is going down.
If caught in a border raid, pray.
In case of war notify the police.
He who chautauquas and runs away may live to chautalk another
    day.
All danger, national and individual, is psychological.
When in doubt do as the Chinaman does—surrender.
Human rights are conserved by preaching sweetness and light.
Hang your latch-key on the outer wall, and the cry "Touch me
    not!"
Force is negative; docility, positive.
In time of peace prepare for more peace.
When an enemy advances toward you seeking your life fling at
    his head a volume of the *Commoner*.

---

* *Life*, August 3, 1916.

Nocturne

It is night.
The thief, eternal representative of humanity, takes up his watch
    on the corner.
The harlot, seeress and sybil, the first born of Life, touches her
    lips with a bit of rouge before she winks for her meal.
The cafes and theatres with their thousand thousand lights begin
    their march on that thingless universe, Ennui.
In the hospitals a vague uneasiness pricks the bodies of the sick
    and thoughts like black parasols open in their heads.
In faultless evening dress the millionaires, yogis of the flesh,
    march up and down a thousand Peacock Alleys seeking their
    undulating Nirvanas.
A poet, who fears the landlord more than the great God, lights
    his globeless burner and begins a marvellous ode to the
    Renoir of Heaven.
A beggar, from whose eyes Hunger has gelded courage, begs a
    coffee from a rich madame, whose heroic courage has forever
    put her beyond the reach of Hunger.
The Moon, mummied in eternal sleep, the frozen Tear of the
    Earth, climbs the ladders of space in the East like a sneak.
It is night, and the multi-eyed, all-peering It comes out of its
    subtle day-sleep to watch the underworld of humans.

---

* *The Rhinebeck Gazette*, August 26, 1916.

On Coney's Beach

Red head, white head,
    Children of the sands!
Freckle mug, pudgy mug
    Out of many lands!

Bloused kids, doused kids
    Dancing in the brine!
Fat kids, thin kids,
    With noses all a-shine!

Laughing babies, crying babies,
    With sashes all a-trail!
Happy babies, baby babies,
    With shovel and with pail!

* *Judge*, August 12, 1916.

"Let Us Have Peace"

The Sunset massed its bleeding swords against the marble turrets
    of the Tomb
Whereon is graven the "Let Us Have Peace" of the warrior who
    sleeps below,
And in that welter of fading fire and invading shadow
I beheld a vision.
In the air, above the cupola, I saw a giant eagle
Whose talons gripped a hawk, and who in turn carried a chicken
    in its beak.
The chicken held in its mouth a worm, a slender worm, a worm
    out of the deep earth,
That clutched with the clutch of fatality a man, whose every
    nerve had been moulded
In the murder-mills of the Struggle for Existence.
And the letters of "Let Us Have Peace" turned to gutters of blood
    before my eyes,
And a Face, ravaged with sinister-smiling wrinkles,
Gleamed in the sun, now a huge red fire-ball sinking behind the
    Palisades.
It was Apollyon, the Holy Ghost of Truth.

* *Life*, August 3, 1916.

Morning Magic

Away! Away!
The hour is struck
On the golden tocsin over the hill
Day is dawning
The flush of the morning
Mantles the dale and fires the rill!

Away! Away!
Night is fled
Into its cellar down in the West,
The dew is a-gleaming,
Broken the dreaming
Of the lark in the hollow and the bird in its nest!

Away! Away!
Alborak is waiting
For my chimeric flight to the Ulbra Place.
Ere the new light dies,
Ere the morning flies
His hoofs will flash in the Night of Space!

---

* *Harrisburg Star-Independent,* September 11. 1916.

Chatterton

Words that were like melodious flutes at the lips of the Soul,
Uremembered of the Earth,
Are printed in the Book of Elohim
And are read by epiphanous beings in unmaterial spaces.

* *The Washington Times*, December 5, 1916.

The Inevitable

To the eye of the child it is a horizon sunken beneath the horizon,
As yet unseen, unapprehended, unguessed.
But as the years snow their flaked and filmy dreams upon Man's brain,
Where he watches them dissolve like luminous gems in vitriol,
The Inevitable, like a fabulous buzzard forever hungry for a Gettysburg or a Marne,
Sweeps around his spirit in hour-narrowing circles like a prodigious lasso,
Or remains poised and motionless over his head like a vulture a-roost in the air,
Where it waits with the patience of the Sun for the Earth.

* *Life*, December 7, 1916.

Ruins

His eyes like two frozen seas epitomized and locked in horizons
 of flesh,
His frigid brow like the high scroll of Eternity (that enormous
 minute that has no seconds),
His impervious dreams
And inviolable visions
A set and fixed ruin on the scoff of his lip—
He, the Poet, Vulcan of the exquisite, like an unsigned and
 desolate god awaited the inexorable minute of putrefaction.

* *The Washington Times*, December 8, 1916.

The Masses

The masses! The masses.
Strangled sigh that goes into the Infinite,
Billion-eyed being that sees nothing,
Whose life is nothing,
Pawns of Fate and candidates for Oblivion.
They manure the glory of the Great
And feed the eagles of the conquerors
And are sap and bone in the body of Genius.
Dragging the chariots of Charlemagne, Caesar and Napoleon
Into the Empyrean of the human imagination,
They fall back into the gaping graves of the Old Mother,
And are like a tale that has never been told.

---

* First published in *Puck*, December 9, 1916; also reprinted in *The Desk Drawer Anthology* (New York: Doubleday, Doran & Company, 1938), p. 77..

Harlequin's Confession

I have driven the light from the day
    And purged the night of its dark,
Cancelled the beams in the Milky Way
    In a fine metaphysical lark.

* *Puck*, December. 9, 1916.

My Golden Age

How long it was after my death I know not—
But it was at the time when the poles of the Earth began to thaw.
At the time when the patchy blood spots on the breastplates of
    my soul were turning to gold
And when the seas of the dead began to give up their living and
    the Coxswain of the Stars dipped his oar no more in the
    Running Seas...
'Twas at that time, I think, I came into my heritage and reaped
    the whirlwind of my joys.

---

* *The Washington Times*, February 6, 1917.

The Risen Giant!

Like the pounding of vast thundercloud waters
'Gainst the mountains and cliffs that circle the world,
The footsteps of a giant, weary of insult, are heard in the West!

His hair is unkempt, but his eyes are like unto
Two conflagrant suns set in the head of the demi-god Hercules
As he strides from the Sierras to the peaks of the East to meet the
    Sultan of Hell!

Now the ears of a world stand a-prick and a-wonder
As against the westering spaces rises the avenger
Clad in muscle and anger.

And there is heard in the night the furious death-croak
Of the tired black eagles of Prussia
That roost in the helmet of the Sultan of Hell!

* *The Washington Times*, February 7, 1917.

The Poet-Burglar

I stood upon the summit of the running seas
And with my iron knuckles, vengeful and predatory,
I shivered the great bulk windows of Space,
Wherein the Merchant of Life and Death exhibits his planets,
    suns and moons.
Some drowsy and half-besotted gods, taking their snooze in the
    ether,
Came full to life, for I had drenched them with blood from a
    gashed artery in my arm;
And they pursued me with a hue and cry adown the ladder of the
    waves,
Glimpsing the booty from my bulgy pockets—
Pursued me, sounding their vast alarm from nadir to zenith,
Into Domdaniel, that "fence" for the reception of stolen stars and
    pilfered dreams
Which stretches away, acre upon acre, under the floor of the
    oceans,
Where they lost me in the meshes of my laughter.

---

   * *The Washington Times*, June 13, 1917. Published first as "The Policeman: A Fable" in
Puck, February. 24, 1917.

Sleep

I am Sleep,
Gray nimb of death,
Impresario of hushed spectacles,
Sculptor of trans-earthly colossi
That I work with thumb and forefinger in the plasms of your
    brain.

Now I woo you to the infoliate depth of my utter shadow,
And you who were chin-deep in time and brain-deep in eternity
Float at the bottom of a waveless sea toward vortices of silence.

The pomp and fascinating necromancy of the invisible Cagliostro
That you called the world
And the hooded and noiseless ghosts that held parliament in
    your arteries
That you called your self
Are immigrant, with all their tinsel and their goods, to
    Nullibiety.

For I am Sleep, the landless ocean,
Sinister aquarium of the dead.

---

* *Life*, March 8, 1917.

March Winds

From the four corners of earth I come,
Battering, ramming, throwing dust in your eyes,
Tangoing up and down Broadway, beating my way to Frisco!

From the four corners of heaven I come,
Whisking the waters into the air, smashing the weather vanes,
Hurling some tiles on the heads of pacifists, chanting a horrible
    doggerel!

From the four corners of the seas I come,
Cooing and lunging, stabbing, meouling like a cat.
Scolding you, bullying you, pounding out April,sculpting the
    miracles of a marvelous Junetime!

* *The Washington Times*, March 11, 1917.

Sub Specie Eternitatis

I hold the stars in my fist
And zodiacs glow on my breast,
My breathing's the ethnic mist
Where men and gods swirl at my hest.

My wrath is the whirlpool of nations,
My smile the re-risen Light.
My eyes are the beds of creations.
My heartbeats the thunders of Might.

I gleam and I shine in the darkness,
I am shadow at the bosom of day,
I stand in your heart in my starkness—
I am nowhere, yet here and for aye!

* *The Washington Times,* April 28, 1917.

The Eternal Avatar

I am sowing seeds of life with the bodies of the brave,
I am sealing up the Past in a planetary grave
I shall use the blood of races on the Palette of my will,
I shall sculpt another Dios with the brains of those I kill—
    For I am Liberty the alchemist, and
    Man is my retort!

I was nailed high in the Caucasus, where my faith hung by a hair;
But I lived to sound the tocsin in Independence Square.
They have inured me in foul dungeons, sealed up with seven seals,
But my spirit smote the Pharaohs and laid in dusty Bastilles—
    For I am Liberty the Phoenix, and
    I die to resurrect!

Now across the seas they call me to a Europe raped and riven
By the Pharisees of Kultur by their padrones lashed and driven.
They have called me through all ages, and never yet in vain;
Flash the sword and sound the bugle from San Diego up to Maine!
    For I am Liberty the gendarme, and
    I have a warrant for a King!

---

* *The Washington Times*, May 10, 1917. Also published as "The Undying Flame."

Chant of Man, 1917

Play upon me, Lord of Hosts!
Play upon me, Lord of Hell!

Make me sing and make me wail,
Make me bawl and make me pray,
Make me rave and make me curse;
Make a clarion of my heart,
Make a reed-pipe of my brain;
Strike a frenzy from my soul,
Pound the keys of all my being—
Make of me the Sublime Solo!

Play upon me, Lord of Hosts!
Play upon me, Lord of Hell!

---

* *The Washington Times*, May 24, 1917.

The Soul of It All

I am an earthquake that shall obliterate the boundaries of
 nations.
A tempest that shall whirl thrones into graves.
A flame that shall consume the mansions of the greater and the
 lesser gods.
In the charnel houses of vast battlefields I hold wassail;
In the sweatshops of thought I prepare the holocausts of the
 future.
From China to the Aisne I ride the sulphur-snouted steeds of the
 Apocalypse—
For I am that most obvious and implacable of gods, Change.

* *The Washington Times*, June 7, 1917.

Similes and a Query

Like a gorgeous flower that has forced its way through the roof of
  a crypt,
Like a miraculous lightning flash at the zenith of Cimmeria,
Like a magic door set in a cloud-lost wall,
The Brain of Man towers against Arcturus and sends its eternal
  Query against the horizons of Space.

---

* *The Washington Times*, June 22, 1917.

Letter-Boxes

Strapped like martyrs with thongs of iron
To walls of brick and posts of steel,
Their metallic maws heavy with mysterious messages,
They flap their iron lips from day to day,
Hungry and forever unappeased of life.

Green-clad sentinels on the outposts of hope and grief,
Sphinxes that dream of the riddles flung into their hearts,
The letter-boxes stand as things apart, brooding on the fatalities
    of written speech.

* *Life*, July 5, 1917.

Hold Yet a Little While!

France, of genius the mother;
France, to all men a brother;
France, that the Hun seeks to smother—
    Hold a little while!

Souls of many made one,
Pleiades become as a sun,
Miraculous men of Verdun—
    Hold a little while!

Supermen on the Aisne,
Mothers from Var to the Seine,
Workers from Brest to Lorraine—
    Hold a little while!

Torn and bleeding and battered,
Tricolor riven and tattered,
Rheims and Lens gasping and shattered—
    Hold a little while!

Mystical daughter of d'Arc,
Hugo of the Promethean spark,
Shall France go down in the dark?—
    Hold a little while!

Gods out of dreams are they,
Cyclops of an ancient lay,
The truth, the life and the way—
    Hold a little while!

A Giant across the sea
Is coming to set thee free
Or coming to die with thee—
    Hold a little while!

* *New York Sun*, August 12, 1917. Reprinted many times and also published as "France (1789–1918)."

Variations on an Old Theme

He (*tentatively*): Yes?
She (*archly*): No.
He (*fawningly*): Yes-s-s?
She (*recedingly*): No-o-o-o?
He (*caressingly*): Yesss?
She (*coquettishly*): Noooo?
He (*imperiously*): Yes!!!
She (*menacingly*): No!!!
He (*imploringly*): Yyyyes?
She (*subtly*): Nnnno.
He (*cringingly*): Yes?
She (*triumphantly*): No!
He (*finally*): Yes?
She (*wearily*): No.
He-She (*smilingly*): Ynoes.

* *The Smart Set*, vol. LIII, no. 1 (September 1917): 92.

[UNTITLED]

The rattle of dice
In the tincups of the gods
As they gamble for our hearts
In the barrooms of Hell.

The click-click of the perpetual marble
As it whirls on the Wheels of Change
Turned by the hand of the Blind Grouper
In the gambling house of the Unborn.

The drip drip of souls
Measured and eternal
As they seep through their coffins
Into the cellars of Dearth.

* *The Wilmington Dispatch.* February 8, 1918.

The Lady of the Hour

She lifted her veils and said:
"I am thy predestined hour,
The hour thou hast waited for in a thousand futures that are
    passed,
The hour thou didst wait to hear strike on the chimes in the suns,
The ecstatic hour of thy Meridian"

And I looked up from my task and said:
"Lady, shroud thyself in thy veils.
Hour, lie still in the graveyard of thy special day."

Her veils curled round her like smoke around a marble
    monument
As she lay the laurel on my head and whispered "Buddha!"

* *Life*, March 7, 1918.

German Pronouns

I—the State.
We—Gott and me.
You—a victim.
Me—The objective case of myself.
Us—Our sons.
Him—One who fights for me.
They—My enemies.
Thou—The Sultan.
Them—The Americans.
It—My planet, the Earth.

---

* *Judge*, May 11, 1918.

Birth Mannerisms

The *New Republic* was born in a sewing basket.
The *Sun* was born with a dollar in its hand.
The *Times* was born with a beard.
The *Herald* was born with false teeth.
The *Evening Post* was born middle aged.
The *Tribune* was born sucking its thumbs.
The *World* was born with a libel suit tucked under its arm.

* *The Quill*, July 1918.

The Vampire

Vampire of the Beautiful,
I suck the blood from the long red arms of westering suns,
Glut my eye on the stilled dreams of Rubens and Rembrandt,
And at the corner of my lips are the suds of the ikor I have lapped
From the cold veins of sculpted seraphim and Olympian gods.
I lie in sodden rapture on the dewy peak of the world,
My wings folded over my brain, fumed and frenzied with the
    souls of Shelley, Wagner and Poe,
That I have sucked dry.

---

* *The Quill*, July 1918.

To a Great American

Halloo! Halloo! Walt Whitman—
Wherever you are—
There in the rich sun soaked earth of your beloved America,
Or there in the light and scream of a comet,
Or deep in the heart of Our Boys that march with banner and
    sword and song
'Gainst the rotten old dynasties of Europe—
Your America is born! Sleep no more, great prophet of us, bold,
    gray trumpeter of our destiny.

Halloo! Halloo! Old Walt!
Tremendous visionaries of these your States,
Chanter in flame-swept strophes of the Super-Race of the West
That was to scale the last wall of feudalism—
We salute thee, there win your tomb where the Delaware waters
    swash and murmur,
We, your America, born of your vision, accoutred for the Sublime
    Adventure,
Are waiting to clasp *you*, Homer to our unborn Saga!

Halloo! Halloo! gray-bearded god,
Encloser of us, womb of our destiny—
The strongest man in the world,
America,
Is to take for bride the most beautiful woman in the world,
France.
Priest of that wedding, come back like an avatar, as you promised,
Come back to the altar of your beloved,
Old Walt of Camden, America incarnate, Shakespeare of
    Patriots,
King David of Democrats!

---

* *The Sun*, July 7, 1918.

Credo for Eunuch-Pacifists

Grip the fiery Dream!
      Hold it,
      Mold it
On the anvil of the Will!
Grasp the bridle of the Horse,
      Stride it,
      Ride it
Toward the ever-flying stars!
Seize the brimming Goblet,
      Drain it,
      Reign it
O'er the logic of the brain!
Whirl the dervish measure,
      Tread it,
      Spread it
'Till men fall dead of joy!
Sing the Song of the Ego,
      Chaunt it,
      Haunt it
The ear of wombed posterities!
Wreck the social Carryall,
      Fire it,
      Pyre it
And dance upon the moon-high flame!
Forge the blade blasphemous,
      Leap it,
      Steep it
In the quivering heart of Ra!

---

* *The Quill*, July 1918.

Anarch

The Fiery Wing of Prodigious Hate cleaves Wall and Roof and Heaven,
It sweeps the guardian Hells aside and breaks the Dials Seven,
And on my brow there blossoms a brand like that which was given Cain,
And I laugh and sing and chant my Hate in the face of the God of Pain.

* *The Quill*, July 1918.

Arise, Ye Dead!

Miracle day of the dead!
Out of your deep trench bed!
For the terror of death hath fled—
 Debout, les morts!

This is no time for sleep,
Nor trysts with worms to keep
Nor into heaven to creep—
 Debout, les morts!

This is no time to die!
Death is the Huns' ally,
Who in putrefactions spy—
 Debout, les morts!

Let earth her old pod break
And out of their slumbers shake
Those who their siestas take—
 Debout, les morts!

For France, that we all adore,
For Liberty and the Tri-Color;
Dead heroes, Encore! Encore!—
 Debout, les morts!
 Debout, les morts!

---

* *The Evening Public Ledger*, July 18, 1918.

ITALY

Built of the golden mists of the Adriatic
And the azures of Neapolitan heavens,
Immaculate pillar of Carrara holding the snowy Roof of the
    World—
Italy, Our Mother of Vengeance, Italy, Our Lady of Light,
We hurry to thee in thy travail, in this thy Gethsemane hour!

Gorgeous palette of the Titian of the Stars,
Crown-room of the genius of a world,
Tetrarch wearing the triple diadem of Leonardo, Dante and
    Angelo—
Italy, eternal avatar of Beauty and Life,
Hurl thy spear, forged of the heart of Prometheus, at the Caliban
    who sprawls over thy Alps!

Thy dead rise from the Isonzo,
Garibaldi starts from his dust, shirted in cardinal,
Thy immemorial cities are Pole Star to thy longing—
Italy, love-child of Apollo and Aphrodite,
Blot out the Ugliness that crawls from the North!

---

* *Il Carroccio*, August 1918.

The Ball Game

What's the score, Satan?
What's the score, God?
Is this the ninth inning of the Game
Begun in the slime of anterior ages,
Or only the seventh, where we stretch for
A twenty-two inning tie that will end in Utter Darkness?

What's the score, Satan?
What's the score, God?
Our score-cards have blown away
Over the fence of the Visible.
Who made the First Error,
And who is that gigantic slugger,
Slugging out fouls all over the world?

What's the score, Satan?
What's the score, God?
Is't the Second Game of a Double-Header,
When we in the bleachers and we in the grandstands
And all the tired, mud-splattered players
Must begin all over again,
Forgetting the old percentages
And the billions of runners lost in the dirty pool at Second?

What's the score, Satan?
What's the score, God?

---

* *New York Tribune*, September 2, 1918.

The Muses of the Moment

Of dead dreams and antique prophecies,
And hopes o'erburdened with the pack of years;
Of man's ascension to chimeric summits,
And shadowy silhouettes of ironic redeemers;
Of these I chant.

Of immarginate thoughts, grotesque, innominate,
And sadistic impulses of petrified wills;
Of the Eleusian mysteries of Woman's eye,
And the infoliate dramas of her heart;
Of these I chant.

* *The Quill,* October, 1918.

Foch!

And in my vision I saw Sainte Jeanne of Domremy arise from the red waters of the Marne.
And in her great eyes labored the Sons of Light forging a Sword for the fist of France.
And out of the ruins of Ypres I saw Saint George arise, clothed in the hide of his Dragon.
And in his hand was a Spear in which flashed the Lion of Albion.
And out of the sap and the root of Belleau Wood strode Western-born Columbia.
And she held by the barrel a Musket she picked up at Lexington, and the butt of it beat on the Brandenburg Gate.
And I knew by the prodigious Certainty in the eye of the great Marshal of Liberty, he that is named Foch, that the Sword and the Spear and the Musket were not in vain!

* *Life*, November. 4, 1918.

D'Annunzio

Titan of earth and air,
Of Dante and Hugo the heir,
Stamped with an almighty Dare—
    The gods of Valhalla salute thee!

Superman, demi-god, singer,
Gabriele, called the Light-bringer,
Anointed by Dionysiac finger—
    Napoleon and Nelson salute thee!

Triumph of Force and Life,
Red Rose of Vision and Strife,
Spurning the reed and the fife—
    The trumpets of Asgard salute thee!

Shoulder him up the stars
To the realm of the Avatars,
First-born of Venus and Mars!
    The dead of the Marne salute thee!

* *Flying*, Feb 1919.

The Eter-Null

I hollow abysms behind your steps as you march toward the stars,
So that you never shall return to the cosy Earth.
Your Hill of Pleasure is all gully and ravine and unbridgeable
    chasm
Whence no traveller has yet come back.
I am the fatal and destructive rain that seeps through the
    Fragonards on the ceiling of your dreams
The rat in the pantry.
The banana-peel on the Route,
The immortal sneak, Circumstance.

* *The Quill,* June 1919.

"Progress"

The debris of Circles,
The crumble of Lines,
The collapse of Spirals
And the perpetual erasure of algebraic prophecies on the
    blackboard of the Future
By the ghostly hand of the immanent X—
Hast thou not, O Man, thy fill of Reason, the Satirist?

* *The Quill,* August 1919.

Wind

Wind! Wind!
Wind of the snarl and wind of the sob,
Wind of the raucous-murderous lunge,
    Rodin of the clouds,
    Angelo of the sea,
Lash me and lave me and rinse out my brain!

Wind! Wind!
Wind that batters the peak and the pine,
Wind that gambols with the light of the stars,
    Breath of Titania,
    Thunder of Thor,
Swish me and swirl me out of my flesh!

Wind! Wind!
Wind that knocks on the doors of the dead,
Wind that pummels the bergs of the North,
    Lash of a Fury,
    Caresser of daisies,
Grave on my forehead the lustre of Light!

---

* *Life*, August 9, 1919.

The Dream Pocket

I am a tobacco pouch,
Stuffed with a thousand dreams,
Heavy with the magic of reverie.

My shredded treasure is more potent
Than the Seven-Leagued Boot
Or the hat of Fortunatus.

I am the little Castle of Memory and Hope,
The lotus-leaf for the Mouth of old King Care,
The amber pool where poets fish for images.

I am your old tobacco pouch.

* *Judge*, August 23, 1919.

Fantasie

A monstrous black Eunuch with a breech-clout of stars rose out
    of the Abyss.
In his right hand he held an open parasol of red which were the
    mathematical points of the spaces above him.
On the middle finger of his left hand, outstretched before,
    gleamed a ring of bleeding rubies;
And as he walked toward the ecliptic of the Earth I heard a
    rumour in my soul:
"Behold him!—the Final Absurdity, the millennial incarnation of
    the Fantasy of Life!"

*   *The Quill*, September 1919.

Vicariously

My eyes are tired of looking at the things they do not see;
My ears are broken with the sounds they cannot hear;
My heart is swollen with the dolour of the times—
Another drop within this jar would o'erbrim the edge of sanity.

---

* *The Quill,* September 1919.

New York

Magnificent and sepulchral lungs of Death,
Stupendous hammer of Commercialism beating a death-march
    on the skulls of humans,
Vast vomitorium of the nations—
A volcanic belch from me to thee!

---

* *The Quill,* September 1919.

Nocturne: 1920

Papa, mamma and baby sat under the evening lamp.
Papa sorted the raisins.
Mamma measured out the sugar.
Baby was learning the alphabet from the *Home Brew Weekly*.
Outside great billows of unfermented rain swept the streets.
But happiness was brewing in the homes of men.

---

* *Cartoons Magazine*, September 1919.

Threshold

An elfin thought on the marge of my mind,
Like a glittering butterfly flown from a drownéd sky,
Or like a sudden strain of windy music heard at the edge of a
    star—

An elfin thought on the marge of my mind
That touches me with innuendoes of past ecstasies
And whistles from its puckered heart wild airs
Learned in the Bedlams of spiritual unreason.

* *The Sun*, January 11, 1920.

The Sea

I am the Sea,
Sower of lightnings, breeder of rainbows,
Screeching and yowling like a Titan new born.
I rove like a hyena from the cellars of earth
To the plinth of the heavens,
Swinging the starlight in my censers of wind.
I fill up the clouds till they rain on the heavens,
And a word from my mouth makes food out o' humans,
The while I gawp and I rave and I lambaste Gibraltars.
Yea, I and the Sea, the Walt Whitman of elements.

* *The Sun*, January 25, 1920.

Rum's 7 Cardinal Virtues

It interfered with work—therefore it promoted the play instinct.
It made healthy people sick—thereby inculcating the value of health.
It filled the jails Sunday morning—thereby saving thousands from the movie mania.
It wrecked homes—in that way hastening the happiness of those unhappily wedded.
It caused the tongue to wag—thereby promoting truth-telling.
It kept late hours—thereby curing insomnia.
It gave some men "Dutch courage"—which is better than none.

---

* *The Laramie Republican*, January 28, 1920.

Fermentation

Wherever three live people gather the conversation ferments.
Radicalism is nothing but the fermentation of suppressed social needs.
Springtime is the fermentation of sap—in flower, tree and the blood of man.
Great art is the fermentation of ideas.
Bryan himself was, twenty years ago, nothing but the fermentation of his conservative ancestors in his blood.
Whatever is tends to souse!

* *Judge*, February 7, 1920.

Vision

In a sudden I beheld
Long queues of light hanging down the back of Space
From heads hidden in the Fourth Dimension—
Heads, I vow, of the Great Mandarins of some transcosmic China
Who confer eternally, coroner-wise, on our smaller destinies.

*   *The Quill,* May 1920.

The Poet and the Hooligans

A poet started to ramble over the rainbow,
And coming to a narrow strand of prismatic vapors
Which bridged the brinks of two heavens,
He saw two brawny Hooligans rise before him
Who started to give him the count, with their eyes;
But the poet, wise as a child, disappeared into the Void,
For he knew those Hooligans, Circulation and Advertising.

* *The Buffalo Evening News*, November 23, 1920.

Peter Pan

"PETER PAN: Children's Matinee To-day."
I went in abashed, rescinding my years, doffing my brain, waving
    a brave farewell to Matter-of-fact
With the white silk handkerchief of my memories of childhood.
A Garden of Laughter,
Laughter, laughter, and tones that fell like pearls from the magic
    heart of Innocence!
Laughter that was starlight broken into a thousand gurgling rills,
Opals that burst in the air like rockets, spilling their beauty on
    my heart
Laughter that was sunlight shimmering on newly budded
    honeysuckle vines,
The cork of reason drawn out of a bewitched wine bottle, and all
    its bubbled beams for me!
Innocence that mocks life and death and sets us all askew and
    awry!
I put my fingers in my ears to stop my tears, but drew them out
    again
To lave in that Ocean of Laughter,
And now it was a buzz-buzz, the hum of honey-heavy bees
That build their mansions in the hair of Titania,
A music struck from the clashed look in fairies' eyes,
The ultra-violet rays of Sound.
Now Peter flies out into the world, and I hear the Spirit of
    Delight sounding a Valkyrian call to the Never Never
    Land—
Like Light come from a viewless Elsewhere to play its *Ninth
    Symphony* upon the golden clavichords of these baby brains,
Like a prodigious fountain that a-sudden spurts and sings in the
    Prison of the World,
Or like tempests of sunlight matted with stars.
Three hours with the laughter and delight of children,
My years rescinded, and my memories like wild waterfalls that
    set their rounded breasts to an eternal Dawn!

* *Life.* July 22, 1920.

To the Old Soak

I am the Mecca of Sorrows,
The blenched and frozen cheek
On which all tears fall,
The Night unto which
All secret sighs are uttered—
Yet, to-day, I am a Mansion of Revels,
A Hall of Laughing Echoes,
A Mirthful Prometheus—
For a case of Scotch hath been bootlegged unto me
This day!

II.

Man—
Having arrived at mental maturity,
Deciphered all Babylonian bricks,
Cuneiform inscriptions and the Congressional Record,
Having explored the air, the earth,
The sea and the Poles,
Having stacked up billions of books
On oodles of subjects
(Saying nothing of canvas and stone
And Victor Herbert),
Having struck the condor and the eagle with panic,
And printed electric words on the air—
Having done all this and a pile of other things,
In his infinite ennui,
He nuzzles into my hip pocket!
Fantastic Man!

* *Harrisburg Telegraph*, September 12, 1921.

Jugement

J'ai mordu dans l'hostie du Temps—elle était amère.
Les chandelles de la pensée vacillaient en mon esprit—
Je ne percevais plus que la densité de l'obscurité.
Mon âme s'était irritée au contact des lèvres de Tes femmes.

(Bah! c'était un tour de coquin pour essayer de me séduire, moi
    QUI TE TRAQUAIS).
L'effort, l'émotion, la pensée, le songe, le désir—qu'est-ce que tout
cela pouvait bien me faire?
J'étais venu pour juger Tes œuvres, non point pour danser au son
de Tes chalumeaux.

Tu ne peux pas étancher la douleur qui est mienne,
Tu ne peux pas induire au sommeil mon éternel NON.
Je suis en ta présence comme un Dieu,
Aussi las que le Changement, et aussi jeune:
Un rebelle mendiant, un précurseur, un négateur,
Un inventeur de choses étranges, incréées, éternelles.

«Un abattoir dissimulé dans un jardin de roses»
Tel est Ton univers:
C'est ainsi que je le juge.

---

* *L'En Dehors*, June 1923. Translated from "Rejection" (pg. 118).

The Bootlegger's Daughter

I am in love with the bootlegger's daughter.
I have to drink rum, I never drink water.
When I go a-courting,
She is always sorting
The bottles of hooch from bottles of booze,
And I am kept busy hiding the clews.

I am in love with the bootlegger's daughter,
And learning the things I hadn't oughter,
We talk of labels and corks
Instead of bluebells and storks:
She calls me "Red Eye," "Rum Hound" and "Stew,"
While I call her my little "Home Brew."

---

* *Kennebec Journal*, June 7, 1924.

Prélude

Dédie à ceux que repousse
mon Individualisme militant.

Je briserai tout tissu en train sur le métier et je filerai ma lumière et mes ténèbres sur l'univers pour l'en couvrir.

J'abattrai les hautes tours de la pensée et je précipiterai l'arche sociale de l'alliance dans les abîmes de l'Ether.

Je déchirerai la tapisserie de l'illusion et je montrerai à l'humanité sa vie et ses dogmes à la lumière de l'Éternité.

Je suis l'Illicite. Mes assemblées ont été tenues dans l'air humide du matin antique, avant que n'eut claironné le premier cri de la pensée humaine.

Je suis le bâtard d'un Hasard infini qui peut bien jamais ne se reproduire. Du zénith de ma pensée, je ricane et dans la toile de ma conception se précipitent milliards sur milliards de mouches de la terre et de l'éther.

Juché là, je me ris de vous—d'un rire qu'ont glacé les vents boréals de l'Infini, d'un rire que gèle le givre de mon inexorable Ricanement.

À l'entour des bivouacs de vos croyances et des feux de vos exaltations saintes, j'erre et rôde et des embuscades que je dresse, en mon Monde du « par delà…» je décoche de temps à autre une flèche qui déchire vos tentes, ô philistins, et vous fait vous souvenir de moi comme d'un maraudeur caché dans les catacombes, comme d'un pirate à bord d'un corsaire rapide, comme d'un fantôme mystique descendu d'une région éthérique.

Évoquerai-je pour vous les spasmes de torture et les sanglots des mondes depuis longtemps disparus? Ils sont rassemblés sur mon cœur comme les brèches sur le bouclier d'un assiégeant. M'écouterez-vous, moi, qu'ont formé les ions suraigus de l'esprit et de la matière? Prêterez-vous l'oreille au Beethoven de la Négation?

Toutes les illusions tombent comme des cadavres en poussière du haut du gibet de ma Connaissance. Je pèle les cosses de

---

* *L'En Dehors*, December 15, 1930. A translation of "Anathema! Litanies of Negation" (pg. 132). This is not a line-by-line translation, but an abridged rendering of the poem.

l'Espérance jusqu'à ce que le Néant momifié apparaisse dans toute sa nudité.

Je danse sur le catafalque de tous mes rêves; je me mue en chrysalide de songes plus beaux encore; je dirige ma course vers des firmaments inimaginables, où je m'engouffre dans les creusets purificateurs de soleils monstrueux.

Et les dieux se réveillent de temps à autre, jetant leurs filaments aux vents du matin, tissant leurs linceuls dans les crépuscules glacés. Cependant, je sais ce que je sais.

Des arbres edéniques refleurissent et de nouvelles Eves sortent de leurs cavernes, et une myriade de Christs récitent monotonément leur complainte douloureuse, ébranlant leurs Calvaires. Cependant je garde pour moi et mes pleurs et mes ricanements.

O poète, n'as-tu pas aperçu mon empreinte, là-haut, sur la colline de ton imagination la plus élevée? O philosophe, n'as-tu pas distingué ma trace dans ta méditation la plus profonde? N'avez-vous pas distingué celui qui sonne de la trompette par delà les soleils, celui qui doigte la flute du temps?

Combien de fois ai-je suspendu mes audiences dans le Royaume des Sentences? Dans mes antichambres et mes salles d'honneur, ils m'attendaient eux, les ilotes du Hasard, les parvenus de l'Accident, mais je restais dissimulé au dedans de mon palais, enseveli dans mes Pensées.

Il me hélaient du Dehors, jetant des pierres par mes croisées, tous, sans exception: fils de charpentiers, faunes et nymphes, troupes olympiennes, Bacchus et Vénus et Momus, Titans de Weimar et de Francfort et de Camden: tous ils me revendiquaient pour eux, moi, celui qui ne porte pas de chaînes. Mais je n'étais pas là, pêchant les léviathans de l'Éternité au moyen d'un appât extrait de mon cerveau.

Car tous les dieux et tous les sauveurs passent sur ma pensée comme une nuée frivole sur le bleu de l'impassible firmament.

J'ai rançonné chaque atome, cherchant un Dessein; j'ai raclé les feux d'innombrables soleils, cherchant au fond de leurs cendres le secret de leurs flammes; j'ai mêlé mon âme à l'éther translunaire. J'ai toujours et partout rencontré cet Anonyme, que je n'ai jamais pu fixer.

J'ai là, sur la nuque, l'empreinte d'un ineffaçable baiser, laissée par Aphrodite. Et, sur mon front, luit une marque éclatante gravée par Lucifer, l'héritier légitime du Trône. Car, jadis, je suis né de la mer et jadis aussi, j'ai sonné la fanfare de la révolte dans les hauteurs célestes.

Je suis le mystère de la Mémoire, le jeu de patience du Rire, l'arc tendu de l'Expectation, la sève montante de la Passion. Dans l'esprit des hommes, je laisserai les empreintes ineffaçables de mes talons écrasants. Dans leurs cœurs, ces claviers de la douleur, retentiront à jamais et le bourdonnement de mes négations et les doux baisers de ma compassion.

Je m'appelle Protée. Mon âme aujourd'hui est un papillon aux ailes étranges et je me suis posé sur de curieuses murailles. La nuit dernière, j'étais une chauve-souris et un mourant m'avait donné naissance. Demain, je serai l'œil hiéroglytique d'un nouveau-né.

Il est des jours où je suis un cousin qui pique les dieux, actionné par une frénésie de destruction. Il est des crépuscules sinistres où je campe dans l'ombre et où je bivouaque avec des feux-follets.

Mon cerveau est un fantastique ver à soie qui tisse des univers sans lendemain et qu'aucune année n'a engendré ; des rythmes étranges le font vibrer. J'obéis à l'appel de visions ataviques impérieuses, de souvenirs gravés sur le parchemin d'antiques émotions et qui s'illuminent soudainement.

Je suis sans rime, sans raison, dépourvu de sens ; et même de bon sens. Je suis, j'étais, je serai, je vois.

Je suis l'esprit de toutes les révolutions. Je suis la fanfare qui s'élève de la barricade qui se dresse là-bas, en pleine rue. Je suis l'homme ligoté qui veut se débarrasser des sangles de la Restriction. On m'a brûlé avec Giordano Bruno, et fusillé avec Ferrer. Je suis socialiste, anarchiste, individualiste ; je suis le Rêve Dynamique, la bombe qui mine toute puissance cherchant à noyer le feu prométhéen dans la vase des sentines de la routine et de la foi.

Je suis l'une de la chevauchée des walküres wagnériennes. Venez, ô hommes, saisissez-moi aux cheveux, attrapez mes sandales de flamme, suspendez-vous à mes paroles. Au delà des Walhallas, et de tout ce qui a péri, et de toutes les salles de massacres, dans l'infini, dans les infinis, nous chevauchons sur l'écume et sur la hâte de notre volonté tumultueuse.

Qui donc ajoutera une coudée à l'Infini et une minute à l'Éternité ? Moi, par ces deux mots : Je suis.

Le corps, cet auge de chair où le temps fouille, furète, pêche, met en pièces: je ne suis pas cela.—Le soleil congelé de la Raison: je ne suis pas cela.—Le Centre opaque de la lumière universelle: je ne suis pas cela.—La divinité du Bien je ne suis pas cela. Pas plus que le Centre passionné du Plaisir. Je suis le Mystère et le Puits merveilleux, l'Œil fabuleux qui n'est point fixé à un visage, le Millénium de la Transformation.

Je suis un enfer lassé du feu éternel, un ciel fatigué de la béatitude, un olympe vidé de ses dieux.

Je suis un païen qui vomit la vigne, un chrétien qui défèque sur la croix et—chose la plus incroyable qui soit—un juif qui crache sur le Veau d'Or.

Je parle, situé de l'autre côté de la matière. Je nie et je crois ; je ricane et j'aime. Je suis un inconstant et un apostat. Je possède l'unité du Niagara, les bornes de l'éclair, le mouvement rythmé des tremblements de terre.

Vie, ô Vie! Airain, granit inexorable. Chaînes indestructibles de nos éternelles lamentations! Hosanna à la Vie, de ma part, à moi, qui suis le perpétuel hérésiarque cosmique.

L'Aiguillon dans la Chair

Ici, où les forces élémentaires m'encerclent, me caressent, et rassemblent, en les attachant, tous les quartiers épais de ma cité ;
Ici, sur la montagne, sous un ciel bleu-verni, et sous un soleil ardemment séducteur, la guerre du vent contre les feuilles se moque de la force que nous tenons cachée ;
C'est ici qu'est la leçon à apprendre, ici est le Professeur éternel, le Seigneur de la guerre de l'Espace, le père de la Haine et de l'Amour.
Ne hais-je pas d'un amour intense? Mon âme ne se fortifie-t-elle pas dans la bataille?
Mon cerveau est un duel de forces contraires et l'objet de ma lutte m'est plus cher que le chatouillement de l'herbe et le bien-être qui accompagne la dégradation.
Guerre! Guerre! qu'on m'apporte mon casque, mon bouclier et l'épée de l'esprit, le grand Moi tout armé que je cherche et qui toujours, lui, me cherche, est enfermé dans une tour d'os envahie par les mauvaises herbes et les champignons vigoureux et vénéneux des « moi » périmés.
Et ici, agrippé à ces forces élémentaires, je passe un pacte passionné avec mes instincts mutes et brutaux.
Pour attaquer toutes les choses mort-vivantes qui obstruent ma marche vers cette tour d'or, recouverte par l'ivraie, laissée à l'abandon, invisible de l'extérieur ;
Et là, au milieu des vents qui se livrent une furieuse bataille, libérer mon Moi à la lumière du soleil,
Ce moi qui vivre exalté à l'ultime degré, desanglé et transfiguré,
Ce moi, Dieu de tous les Dieux.

---

* *L'En Dehors*, September 1932. Translated from the English "The Quest in the Flesh" (pg. 108).

Rejet

J'ai mordu à l'hostie du Temps—elle n'est pas douce.
Chaque cierge de pensée vacillait en mon âme—et je vis seulement la densité des ténèbres.
Mon âme s'était dissipée aux lèvres de Tes femmes.
(Peuh! c'était folle gageure qu'essayer de me séduire, moi, Ton Poursuiveur.)
Effort, émotion, pensée, rêve, convoitise—qu'est tout cela pour moi?
Je vins pour juger Tes œuvres, non pour danser à Tes pipeaux.

Tu ne peux étancher la peine qui est mienne,
Tu ne peux gagner au sommeil mon Éternel Négation.
Tel un dieu je suis en Ta présence,
Aussi fatigué que le Changement, et aussi jeune;
Mendiant Rebelle, Présage, contempteur,
Inventeur d'étranges choses, incréé, éternel!

Un abattoir dans un jardin de roses—
Tel est Ton univers:
Ainsi donc je juge!

---

* *Simplement Vagabondages*, Novembre-Décembre 1935. Translated from "Rejection" (pg. 118), and is a different translation from "Jugement" (pg. 291).

Ma Passion Sacrée

La passion du marin pour de nouvelles terres,
La passion du navire récemment lancé pour l'écume jaillissante,
　　pour les vagues qui montent aux cieux,
Ma passion est éternelle et sans fin,
Je me tiens dans le cercle de la Terre et je convoite les cercles qui
　　sont au-dessus et au-delà,
Qui s'élargissent tels des nœuds coulants dans les trous d'azur et
　　d'opale,
Jusqu'à ce que mon regard se perde au zénith couronné de feu.
Je convoite avec mes yeux et mes oreilles, concupiscent des choses
　　insoupçonnées, de toutes les choses non encore conquises.
Je convoite la force qui s'élance et me pousse en avant
Et me purge de la boue des vieilles habitudes, collées à moi
　　comme une carapace.
—La force qui pousse la fine aiguille de mon désir exacerbé au
　　travers d'un million de noyaux éphémères
Et la plante au cœur de toute vérité qui s'évanouit.
Mes convoitises me font me raidir et rachètent ma douleur;
Et je soupire et je sanglote et je ris à l'oreille de l'Aimée,
Étendue sur les vents, emprisonnée dans la rafale,
Jusqu'à ce qu'elle capitule et délivre son ultime secret.
Elle, l'Aimée, ma finalité, cible de mes convoitises, épiant ici,
　　guignant là, éternellement perdue et regagnée éternellement:
Je reviens à elle, toujours, sans cesse, sur les flèches du temps.

---

* *L'En Dehors*, August-September 1936. Translated from the English "My Holy Lust" (pg. 112).

CODPIECE

I dance with the Ultimate,
Prance with the Sublimate,
Spurning the Proximate—
>Of Nothing the Knight!

First Jockey on Pegasus,
Trainer of Bucephalus,
The stars are mere detritus
>Under my flight!

The Kalpas of Brahma
Are a toy diorama,
An agate digamma
>On the scroll of my brain!

My minutes are ages,
The gods are my pages,
My valets the Sages—
>But I live in a Drain!

* *Chiron the Centaur, 1937*

Le Dormeur

Mon âme s'était endormie au cœur d'une grande cité, au milieu
    des regards en coin de ses millions d'habitants;
les sabots de fer de maints animaux étranges et monstrueux
    gravèrent leur empreinte sur mon moi prescient et jusqu'alors
    immaculé,
qui gisait roide et anéanti sur les grand'routes du monde.
O mon âme, mon âme, réveille-toi!
Les vagues m'ont recouvert
et des choses rampantes aux yeux ardents se sont faufilées
    jusqu'au trône blanc d'où je régnais,
et chacune des Sept Mortelles Délectations m'a baisé,
et épuisé ma force en me léchant de sa langue polie et jaune.
O mon âme, mon âme, réveille-toi!
Oh ! la terreur de ce sommeil et ce moi effacé, annihilé, fondu
en des choses viles et grossières.
Et cette lente mort de ce moi qui a bu la ciguë de ce monde, qui
    n'amène pas la mort
—la mort, ce point final—
Mais une mort où grouillent des cauchemars abjects—intervalle
    sans oubli... —
O mon âme, mon âme, réveille-toi!
De leurs cryptes s'évadent mes anciens "moi"
Et tandis que je reste là le regard impuissant fixé sur la tête de
    mort,
ils s'insinuent par les petits rivets d'airain de l'habitude jusqu'au
    centre de mon être.
O mon âme, mon âme, réveille-toi!

---

* *L'En Dehors*, March 1937 This is a translation of the poem "The Sleeper" (pg. 115).

Litanies de la Négation

Des myriades d'aeons durant, vous avez semé dans les sillons de l'Avenir, et qu'avez-vous récolté d'autres que des épines et des chardons dont vous tressez des couronnes?

    Vous avez tissé ces innombrables siècles sur les métiers de vos espoirs, et qu'avez-vous obtenu d'autres que vos suaires?

    La glèbe de ce monde est en friche et les navettes du désir sont hantées par des fées adroites et astucieuses, si bien que vous semez et tissez sans résultat.

    Du miraculeux tombeau du passé sortent les épiphanies de vos innombrables demains qui, à leur tour, deviennent des cadavres. Et malgré tout, vous avez soudoyé les maquereaux de cette vieille putain Espérance et vous attendez, à sa porte, et cela, malgré que je vous aie dit et ressassé qu'il ne s'agit là que du cabinet de prestidigitation du Maître!— Moi, l'éternelle Sentinelle et le Contradicteur de votre éternel, moi qui vous aime et licane de vous, du zénith de sa connaissance...

---

*   *L'Unique,* July 1945. A translation of an excerpt of *Anathema! Litanies of Negation.* (pg. 132), the paragraph starting: "You have sowed these myriad..."

The Presence:
Hymn of a Nihilist to Oblivion

> "The mysticism of the
> voluptuous joy of
> Eternal Emptiness."
> —Nietzsche.

I

Being is Thy Space, Will is Thy Time, and all matter and mind is but an atom in the iris of Thy luminous eye, O Presence!

My pain and my pleasure are unknown to Thee as a moth is unknown to the lamp, O Presence!

Black with despair or rubescent with joy, I walk in Thee, O Presence!

Sleeping, I drift in Thee like a blind fish. Waking, I sail the boat of my soul on Thy Being, O Presence!

When I have acclaimed Thee there is no applause. When I have cursed Thee there is no frown, for Thou knowest me not, O Presence!

Thou dost miraculize my days and translate the most familiar objects into the thrill of eternal mystery, O Presence!

II

Thou pourest from all crannies and all nooks of life like light from a hidden Sun.

Thou art like the air through which I walk, unseen, transparent, sustaining.

Thou art behind me and before me, on top of me and under me—a sunken boat am I suspended in the middle of Infinite Waters!

Thou art the wisdom of my ignorance and the culminant beam of my knowledge.

I retreat in Thee and win all battles. I advance in Thee and lose all my gains.

---

*   *Finis*, 1945.

III

My many words and reveries die in Thee, O Presence, like the murmur of muttered dreams in the night.
My frets and hates are caught in Thy glowing laughter like the tears of little children in the sing-song of their mother.
My pride swells in Thee like the imperial rose in the dawn of June—to drop petal by petal into the abysms of Thy eternity.

IV

Good is finite and Evil is infinite. And still, O Presence, Thou knowest naught of these measures.
All that lives must die and dissolve like a dream of fair women on a battlefield. And still, O Presence, Thou knowest naught of these processes.
For, O Presence, Thou art like the sea: perfect evil and perfect good simultaneously. Being both, Thou art neither, O eternally virginal One!

V

Thou art the humor of my tears, the humor of my doubts, the humor of my desires.
I seek to decompose Thee, to analyze Thee in the crucible of my brittle mind—and Thou dost laugh with Thy all-enmeshing Silence.
Silence is the mirth of Thee—silence delicate and 'whelming.
The night is in the Sun, my No is in my Yes, and my little all is in Thee. In the Presence there is no seam.

VI

I lay down my will before the Presence as I lay down my shoes before going into my bed.
I enter Thy abode as Thou dost enter the sea-drops and the dew on the meadow—silently and without motion.
My breath mingles with Thine and my eyes are tiny suns that move in Thy spaceless ether.
Lapped in Thee, I have nothing of self, being the All.

Poet Nears Delectable State
Benjamin DeCasseres, Philosopher, Scans Jersey's Palisades And Pens Dream Words

Few men achieve the ideal; but Benjamin DeCasseres, iconoclastic poet and philosopher, has approached pretty close to that delectable state, although he'd be the first to deny it.

He has a home, the front windows of which "overlook the whole of nature," he has a pleasant study where he can write to his heart's content—mile upon mile of pages—and he is getting his books published.

True, he is publishing them himself and the cost exceeds the returns, but at long last he is getting between the covers his "poor neglected babies without clothes and without a house to live in," and that to DeCasseres is a satisfaction that brings balm to his heart and peace to his soul.

World Waits Eye

It is a great thing to be a poet; it enables you to see any picture your heart desires from whatever point you happen to be.

"Look," says DeCasseres, "from my sun-swept balcony I can look out over the entire world; all nature is spread before me."

"Yes," adds the equally poetic but more logical Mrs. DeCasseres, "and sometimes when we look out there is a battleship anchored almost at our door."

Which means that DeCasseres' outlook on "all nature" is an apartment on Riverside drive, squarely facing the Hudson river and the Jersey shore. It appears rather urban to non-poetic eyes, what with apartment buildings, bridges, an automobile-choked street, advertising signs, tugboats and railroad trains.

Reason Last Refuge

But, as DeCasseres has well said: "Reason is the last refuge of a poet—the frost in the garden of dreams." So between the urban lines DeCasseres reads what is written in a stretch of blue water, the ageless Palisades of Jersey, the trees, the grass, and sometimes

---

* *The Arizona Republic*, Sun, Jan 31, 1937. Authorship attributed to the Associated Press.

a few flowers—and that to the poet is enough for the "whole of nature."

And at night after the wan winter sun has dropped beyond the Jersey shore and a million lights come out on both sides of the water, DeCasseres is up in the heavens somewhere seeing a million suns flashing in the sidereal universe—a modernistic universe in which the time of night is flashed every two minutes by an enterprising clock manufacturer.

In "Operating Room"

With this scene for inspiration, DeCasseres returns to his study, brilliantly lighted—"like an operating room," says Mrs. DeCasseres—and pens his cosmic philosophies.

He's already published more than a score of volumes and contributed to as many more—but his writing piles up faster than he can get it between covers. As a result, he has a closet full of manuscripts, including his own "spiritual and intellectual autobiography," a record of his inner thoughts through many years.

The study is lined with pictures and mementoes of the great, with bookcases containing the works of those authors to which he feels a spiritual affinity—Spinoza, Emerson, Maeterlinck, Baudelaire, Montaigne, Blake, Whitman, Schopenhauer and Nietzsche.

Practical Joker

There is a copy of H. L. Mencken's last revision of "The American Language," inscribed "To Benjamin DeCasseres—arch-enemy of the atom."

On the mantle is Mencken's "Maryland Mad Stone," one of the Baltimore sage's practical jokes. Let DeCasseres tell of it.

"This package came through the mail one day with no indication as to what it contained. I had been writing against Communism and my first thought was that it was a bomb. 'This is the end of DeCasseres,' I said.

> I listened for hidden ticks; then I put it near a bucket of water ready to douse it. For two hours I debated what to do about the thing. Then I decided to throw caution to the wind and open it.

So what? Out pops this crazy boulder with a card attached—a printed card from the "Maryland State Board of Mad Stone Examiners," and signed by Mencken as "inspector."

That Mencken is one of the world's most diligent practical jesters is known full well to his friends. DeCasseres and others often get letters in which are enclosed some printed piece of foolishness, such as the advertisement for the "Kosher Chop Suey Saloon."

Earlier pictures and cartoons of DeCasseres depict him in satanic form—probably to match the satanic barbs from his pen.

Nowadays, despite his literary thunderbolts, he appears absolutely cherubic—with a rounded, kindly, smiling, youthful and thoroughly serene face, the face of a man who accepts the world at its face value.

Probably he has forgotten that he once wrote: "The deadliest weapon in the world is a good-natured smile," or maybe he is just living up to it.

Philosophy Is Easy

At home, he seldom gets out of his dressing gown, and his personal philosophy of life is worn with the same comfortable ease as that dressing gown.

In fact, what DeCasseres writes and what he lives appear to be in two different dimensions.

"As a man I scorn the gods; as a god I scorn men," he has recorded.

But he'll make a friend warmly welcome and beam beatifically through the conversation.

He radiates perfect contentment, but writes thus of the same state of being:

"Perfect contentment is like a full purse in the desert."

He lives in perfect harmony with his surroundings, but again says: "Whatever is perfect is in a museum."

Unruffled Love? No!

His own love story—his wife is a granddaughter of an Indian princess—is a dramatic and appealing one; its history is recorded in a book, *Love Letters of a Living Poet*.

Yet he has written: "Perfect, unruffled love can only exist between two imbeciles."

Probably a more truthful statement would be his epigram, "Women and music should remain forever misunderstood."

DeCasseres considers himself a prophet, but of seers in general he has said: "A prophet is a man with an abnormal memory." By this token he can't agree with himself.

DeCasseres has some pretty positive ideas about any number of things, but has said in print: "There is no adventure like finding yourself continually wrong in your judgments."

Has No Enemies

He has friends galore; no known personal enemies. This happy state may have inspired these statements: "What makes friendship so desirable is that one does not have to love one's friends; it is only necessary to be friendly."

"Success is the art of being polite to the people you hate."

Some one recently made a slurring allusion to him in print.

"Can I sue him for libel?" DeCasseres asked a lawyer friend.

"Yes, if you can prove you're not what he says," was the reply.

So DeCasseres smiled and added the clipping to the hundreds of others that have been written about him.

Dealing in irony, he sadly admits the average man does not understand this nuance of language. But he believes in the high purpose of irony, as per:

Wears Collar Of Irony

"To prevent the head from falling toward the ground in despair wear the high collar of irony." And so he does. It permits him to record observations such as these:

"Hope is a saving bank run by swindlers."

"Belief of any kind is impossible without some degree of intolerance."

"Perpetual tragedy of a few: To be at large in one's own skull."

"Every great poet should have a beggar's license."

"There are many who believe themselves wise who are merely ill."

"Talent is an infinite capacity for imitating genius."

"The first superwoman will be she who tells the photographer: 'Photograph me just as I am!'"

"The truth can only be made plausible by making it look like a lie."

"Commonplace things are things that no genius has yet looked at."

Stirs Up Cosmos

"Tell a woman you understand her and she may love you; but if she discovers that you really do understand her she will hate you."

"That which all agree is true is of no interest."

"Each tomorrow brings us closer to yesterday."

"Every lie has two sides—the logical side is called the truth."

"Each one lives behind a statue of himself; he calls it the ideal."

"Humility: to be prouder of the black eye you got than of the one you gave."

And so DeCasseres goes on, stirring up the cosmos, inventing epigrams, evolving paradoxes, blowing hot, blowing cold—and smiling cherubically all the while. But those who really know him think he has summed up himself rather neatly in this epitaph:

"When they excavate me they will find my teeth buried in my heart."

INDEX

This index gathers more than a thousand entries drawn from across the imaginative and intellectual terrain of *IMP: The Collected Poetry of Benjamin DeCasseres*. It serves chiefly as a guide to names, titles, and places—real, fictional, mythological, and historical—that appear throughout the text. Poem titles are listed both where they occur and where they are referred to. Personifications such as *Death* are treated as proper names, while abstractions like *Time* are left aside.

Entries for DeCasseres himself, and for the many invocations and epithets of "God," have been purposefully omitted, as their repetition would obscure rather than clarify the poet's intricate web of reference. Likewise, the titles of the poetry volumes from which these works are drawn have been excluded, since their inclusion would add little to the reader's navigation or understanding.

"[untitled]" 261

Abyss 87, 144, 166, 186, 279
Achilles 234
"Across the Gulf" 36, 233
Adriatic 270
Aerschot 35, 223
Aeschylus 63, 67
Agamemnon 234
"A Gray Minute" 38
Ahriman 47, 143
Aisne 256, 259
Albert & Charles Boni 20, 21
Alborak 215, 242
Aldebaran 126, 227
"The Alleys of Eld" 116
Alps 270
Amazon 214
America 26, 33, 34, 38, 45, 55, 56, 59, 60, 263, 266
American Library Service 23, 55

The American Mercury 15
"An Anarch Minute" 38
"Anarch" 37, 38, 268
Anarch 16
"Anathema!" 133, 302
Andes 198
Angelo 270, 277
"An Incident" 31, 211
Antwerp 223
Aphrodite 142, 147, 171, 270
Apollo 5, 47, 137, 143, 241, 270
Ararat 196
Archy and Mehitabel 19
Arcturus 152, 191, 257
Ariel 5
"Arise Ye Dead!" 38, 269
The Arizona Republic 44,
Armand, E. 16, 30, 31, 40
Asgard 274
"A Son of God" 181
Aspasia 143
Astoreth 119

Athalie 33
Athens 215
Attila 168
Aurelius 168
"Ave, Zarathustra!" 186

Babylon 290
Bacchus 136, 140
Bach, Johann Sebastian 38
"The Ball Game" 271
Balzac, Honoré de 30, 46, 63
Banu, Constantin 219
Barclay, Rev. Dr. 68
Bastille 170, 254
Bataille, Georges 26
Baudelaire, Charles 62, 136, 306
Bedlam 283
Beethoven, Ludwig van 38, 135, 165
Belgium 223
Belial 144
Belleau Wood 273
Bellerophon 49
Beyond-Man 46, 137, 138
"Beyond Sense" 89
Billings, William 30
"Bio" 31, 214
"Bird Of The Night" 104
"Birth Mannerisms" 37, 264
"Birth of a Sword" 232
Blackstone Publishers 62
Blake, William 47, 62, 192
Blenheim 144
Bluebell 199
Bodenheim, Maxwell 18
The Bookman 26, 62
Book of Elohim 188, 243
"The Bootlegger's Daughter" 39, 292

Borgia 221
Brahma 300
Brahmapootra 139
Brandenburg Gate 273
Brest 259
Brown University 33
Brussels 223
Bryan 286
Bucephalus 300
Bucharest 35
Buddha 47, 168, 262
The Buffalo Evening News 288
Byron, Lord 38

Caceres, Samuel de 45
Caesar 199, 206, 234, 246
Cagliostro 107, 168, 251
Cain 154, 165, 268
Caliban 96, 270
California 62, 66
Calvary 139
Camera Work 15, 30
Carmel 62, 63, 67, 68
Carrow, David 68
Cartoons Magazine 282
Casseres, Miriam de (nee Spinoza) 45
Caucasus 193, 254
Chameleon 47
"Change and an Ending" 107
"Change and Ending" 23
"Chant of Man, 1917" 255
Charlemagne 246
"Chatterton" 36, 243
Chatterton, Thomas 25, 36
Chicago Literary Times 18
Childe Harold's Pilgrimage 38
Chimborazo 183
Chimera 49, 145, 164, 171
"Chimeras" 164

311

China 256, 287
Chiron the Centaur 40, 300
Chopin 62, 194
Christ, Jesus 47, 49, 90, 139, 143, 162, 168, 191, 224, 230
Cimmeria 110, 257
"The Cleft In The Wall" 105
"The Closed Room" 99
"The Coast-Range Christ" 63, 64, 68
Cobb, Osiris 41
"Codpiece" 40, 300
Colossus 70
Columbia 273
Columbus, Christopher 30, 191, 205
Commoner 238
Concord School 59
"The Conquerors" 36, 234
Cosmopolitan 16, 30, 205
"Credo for Eunuch-Pacifists" 267
Crowley, Aleister 30
Cubism 15, 17
Cupid 147
Current Opinion 28
Cuse, Jack 5, 18
Cyclops 259
"The Cynic of Nazareth" 38, 90

Dada 17
"D'Annunzio" 274
D'Annunzio, Gabriele 30, 38, 46
Dans la tourmente 33, 216
Dante 62, 270, 274
d'Arc, Joan 259
"Dawn" 176
"The Dead Who Live" 23, 85
Death 53, 75, 117, 148, 149, 161, 164, 168, 177, 194, 195, 235, 251, 281
de Caceres, Samuel. *See* Caceres, Samuel de
DeCasseres, Adele "Bio" 23, 31, 40, 110, 306
de Casseres, Miriam. *See* Casseres, Miriam de
DeCasseres, Walter 24, 25
"The Decoy" 161
de Fornaro, Carlo. *See* Fornero, Carlo de
de Gourmont, Rémy. *See* Gourmont, Rémy de
de Lautréamont, Comte. *See* Lautréamont, Comte de
Delaware 266
Delilah 143
"De Profundis" 91
Der Krieg (painting) 36, 234
de Unamuno, Miguel. *See* Unamuno, Miguel de
de Zayas, Marius. *See* Zayas, Marius de
The Dial 21
El Diario 15
Dionysius 19, 35, 60, 69, 215, 223, 274
Discussion 16
Domdaniel 250
Don Juan 154
Don Quixote 5, 48
Dore, Gustav 62
Dostoyevsky, Fyodor 48, 49, 62, 63
"The Dream Pocket" 278
"Dying" 84

Earth 166, 188, 195, 239, 243,

244, 248, 263, 275, 279
East and West 18
Eden 139
The Egoist 5
Einstein, Albert 31
The Elect and the Damned 62
Eleusian mysteries 272
Elysia 215
Emerson, Ralph Waldo 30, 36, 46, 306
Epicurus 21, 139
Erinys 221
Érynnie 33
"The Eternal Avatar" 254
The Eternal Return 47
"The Eter-Null" 275
Ethiope 162, 224
The Letters of Robinson Jeffers 24
Eumeswil 38
Europe 215, 254, 266
Eve 139, 165
The Evening Kansan-Republican 204
The Evening Public Ledger 269
"Exvolved" 86

"Face To Face" 96
"Facts" 172
"Fantasia" 166
Fantasia Impromptu: Finis 20, 36, 40
"Fantasie" 39, 279
Father of Lies 77
"Fauna" 69
"Fermentation" 39, 286
"Fifty!" 36, 237
Finis 40, 303
Flacăra 35, 219
Flanders 223

Flaubert, Gustave 34
Flying 38, 274
"Foch!" 273
Foch, Ferdinand 273
Ford, John 67
Fornaro, Carlo de 2, 15, 20, 73
Fortunatus 278
Forty Immortals 41, 45, 46, 47
Fragonard 275
France 31, 215, 259, 266, 269, 273
"France (1789–1918)" 259
Franklin, Benjamin 30, 205
Free Verse. *See vers libre*
Furies 195

Gabriele 274
Galileo 30, 205
"The Gallic Lark and the Sow-on-the-Rhine" 31, 215
Gambrinus 61
Ganges 139
Gautama 2, 76, 136
Genealogy of Morals 51
Genghis Khan 234
"German Pronouns" 263
Gethsemane 73, 270
Gettysburg 244
Gibraltar 284
"The God of Negation" 87
"Godward" 88
Golden Calf 147
Goldman, Emma 15
Golgotha 63
Gotham Book Mart 26
Gourmont, Rémy de 33, 35, 46, 48, 216, 217
Goya 234
Great Crossways 96
The Greensboro Daily News 232

Greenwich Village 37

"The Hague—1915" 228
"Half-Seen" 100
Hamlet 5
Hannibal 234
Hapsburg 226
Hardy, Thomas 46, 48, 62, 63, 64
Harlequin 192
"Harlequin's Confession" 247
The Harrisburg Star-Independent 242
The Harrisburg Telegraph 290
Hartmann, Eduard von 51
Hartmann, Sadakichi 15
"The Haunted House" 162, 224
Havel, Hippolyte 15, 16, 35
Haywood, Bill 36
Hearn, Lafcadio 62
Hecht, Ben 18
Hegel 195
Helena 129, 171
Hell 150, 214, 221, 226, 249, 255, 261
Herbert, Victor 290
Himalayas 152
Hippogrif 173
Hohenzollern 226
"Hold Yet a Little While!" 259
"Home" 128
Homer 266
Hors du troupeau 30, 207
Howard, Robert E. 36
Hubbard, Elbert 15
Hudson River 305
Hugo, Victor 35, 274
"The Humorist" 175, 231
Huneker, James Gibbons 38
Hunt, Ernest M. 6

Iago 68, 175, 221
Ibsen, Henrik 48
"The Ideal" 182
Il Carroccio 38, 270
"Imagination" 170
"Immune" 129
"In an Old-Time Tavern Booth" 7, 18
"The Inevitable" 244
"Ingression" 198
The International 30, 208, 209, 210, 211, 212, 213, 214
"In the Adytum" 23, 109
"In the Backyard of Life" 167
"In the Ramble" 236
"In the Slums" 31, 212
Iron Guard 35
Isis 77
Isonzo 270
"Italy" 38, 270
Italy 270

Japan 172
Jeffers, Robinson 19, 24, 25, 62, 63, 65, 67, 69, 70
Jewish People's Institute of Chicago 18
"Jews as Literary Idealists" 38
Jezebel 143, 209
Job 58
Judas 191
Judge 36, 40, 240, 263, 278, 286
"Jugement" (Fr) 291, 298
The Juggernaut 5, 18
Jünger, Ernst 38
Jupiter 193

The Kansas City Star 237
"Keats" 171

Keats, John 171
Kennebec Journal 292
King David 226
Kishinef (Chişinău) 228

Labadie, Laurance 16
"The Lady of the Hour" 262
"L'aiguillon dans la Chair" (Fr) 297
Laïs 143
"L'Alouette Gauloise et la Truie du Rhin" 31, 216
The Laramie Republican 285
"Late Autumn" 210
Lautréamont, Comte de 26
La Vie Parisienne 5
Leaves of Grass 52
Le Dormeur (Fr) 301
L'En Dehors 16, 31, 291, 293, 297, 299, 301
Lens 259
Leonardo 270
Leopardi, Giacomo 27, 136
Le Revue des Deux Mondes 5
Les Chants de Maldoror 26, 34
Les Châtiments 35, 223
Les Forces Tumultueuses 223
Les Soirs 223
"Letter-Boxes" 37, 258
"Let Us Have Peace" 241
Lexington 273
Life 5, 231, 238, 241, 244, 251, 258, 262, 273, 277, 289
Light-bringer 274
Lilith 165
Liszt, Franz 211
"Litanies de la Négation" (Fr) 302
London 225
"The Long Vigil" 101

Lorraine 259
Louvain 35, 223
"Love and Sleep" 94
Love Letters of a Living Poet 23, 24
"Love the Destroyer" 23, 53, 117
Lucifer 77, 96, 141, 142, 170, 194
Lucretius 27, 136
L'Unique 302
Lynchburg 29
Lyra 147, 169

Maeterlinck, Maurice 46, 48, 306
"Magical Night" 165
Maine 254
"Man" 168
"Ma Passion Sacrée" (Fr) 299
"Marche Funebre" 163
"March Winds" 252
Marne 228, 244, 273, 274
Marquis, Don 7, 17, 18, 19, 23, 45, 56, 57, 58
Mars 274
"Masque of the Minutes" 28, 190
"The Masses" 246
Maya 143, 153, 173
Mayfield, John S. 62
McIntyre, Oscar Odd 37
Mecca 138, 160, 182, 290
Medusa 5, 168
Menelaus 234
Mercure de France 5, 31, 33, 217
Messalina, Valeria 143
Mexico City 15
Milky Way 87, 247
Milton, John 38
The Mind 30

"Miracles" 183
Mirbeau, Octave 36
Modern Poetry Little Magazine Collection 29
Momus 140
Monahan, Michael 15
Mona Lisa 67
Montaigne, Michel de 306
Mont Blanc 123
Moon 107, 119, 123, 143, 152, 153, 160, 162, 164, 175, 182, 184, 195, 197, 224, 231, 239, 250, 267
"Morning Magic" 36, 242
"Moth-Terror" 111
Motion Picture Herald 15
Much Ado 5
Mumbo-Jumbo 144
Munchausen 159
The Muse of Lies 47
"The Muses of the Moment" 272
Mussolini, Benito 31
"My Comic Perspective" 77
"My Divine Hate" 81
"My Golden Age" 24, 36, 248
"My Holy Lust" 112, 299
"My Lamp" 213
"My Shadows" 23, 97
"The Mysterious Weaver" 35, 225

Napoleon 88, 168, 183, 246, 274
Narragansett Pier 62
The Nation 27
Navire d'Argent 31
Nazareth 90
Neapolitan 270
Neihardt, John G. 27
Nelson 274

Neptune 184
Nero 33, 162, 222, 224
Never Never Land 289
The New Era-Lancaster 203
New Jersey 305
"New York" 39, 281
New York City 15, 19, 23
The New York Evening Post 264
The New York Evening Sun 28
The New York Herald 264
The New York Journal-American 43, 44
The New York Letter 37
The New York Sun 16, 30, 223, 225, 227, 233, 236, 259, 264, 266, 283, 284
The New York Times 27, 39, 264
The New-York Tribune 33, 215, 264, 271
The New York World 33, 264
Nietzsche, Friedrich 16, 17, 21, 27, 30, 31, 36, 46, 48, 49, 51, 60, 69, 70, 193, 195, 303
"Night Cometh" 229
Ninth Symphony 289
Niobe 190
Nirvana 76, 162, 224, 239
"Nocturne" 239
"Nocturne: 1920" 282
Nosferatu 15, 38
Novalis (Georg von Hardenberg) 45

Old Care 84
The Old Soak: and, Hail and Farewell 7
Olympia 265
Olympus 140, 147
"On a Marriage" 53, 92

"On Coney's Beach" 36, 240
O'Neill, Eugene 19, 26, 59
Oppenheim, James 55
Ormuzd 47, 143
Orpheus 165
Others 28, 224
"The Overlord" 159
Overman. *See* Beyond-Man
"The Overone" 113

"The Pacifist's Breviary" 238
Paine, Thomas 36
Palisades 241, 305
Pan 198
Panzas, Sancho 48
Paphos 211
The Papyrus: A Magazine of Individuality 30
Paraclete 159, 162, 224
Paradise Lost 38
The Paris Times 31
"Pater Noster" 33, 221
"Pater Noster" (Fr) 217
"Pater Noster" (Ro) 219
Peacock Alley 239
"The Peeper" 78
Pegasus 300
"Peter Pan" 289
Pharaoh 254
Pharisees 254
Philistia 134, 138, 146
The Philistine 15
Phoenix 254
"The Pickpocket" 178
Pierrot 159
Pittsburg 62
Pleiades 164, 259
Plotinus 192
Poe, Edgar Allan 52, 62, 194, 265

"The Poet and the Hooligans" 288
"The Poet-Burglar" 250
The Poetry Journal 18, 51
Point Joe 62
Point Lobos 62
"Potporri" 226
"Prayer" 30, 205
"Pre-Destined" 127
"Prélude"(Fr) 293
"The Presence: Hymn of a Nihilist to Oblivion" 40, 303
Priapus 140
"Progress" 276
Prometheus 47, 57, 96, 138, 154, 168, 193, 226, 259, 270, 290
"Prophetic" 102
Prospero 227
"The Protagonist" 73
Protopopescu, Dragoş 35
Prussia 249
Psalms 60
Puck 5, 40, 144, 170, 173, 246, 247, 250
Pythagoras 154, 162, 195, 224

"The Quest in the Flesh" 108, 297
The Quill 6, 37, 38, 39, 264, 265, 267, 268, 272, 275, 276, 279, 280, 281, 287

Ra 267
Rabelais 199
Racine, François 33
Rand, Ayn 19, 44
Randolph, Lewis Carter 29
Reflex 18
"Rejection" 118, 291, 298

"Rejet" (Fr) 298
Rembrandt 265
Renoir, Pierre-Auguste 239
"Resolved" 123
"Resurrection Night" 103
"Revelation" 31, 209
Revolt 16, 35, 36, 226, 228, 229, 230
Revue des Deux Mondes 31
Rheims 259
Rhine 223
The Rhinebeck Gazette 239
Ridgeway, Ann N. 24
Riga 234
Rimbaud, Arthur 25
"The Risen Giant!" 249
"Roan Stallion" 63, 67, 69
"Robinson Jeffers: Tragic Terror" 19
Rodin, Auguste 30, 63, 277
Romanoff 226
Rome 64
Ronsard 215
Rosinante 170
"The Rotted Ideal" 82
Rubens, Peter Paul 265
Rudens, S.P. 18
"Ruins" 24, 36, 245
"Rum's 7 Cardinal Virtues" 39, 285
Russia 226

Sahara 206
Sainte Jeanne of Domremy 273
Saint George 273
Salamis 144
"Salutation" 197
Salvation Army 7
San Diego 254
Sanger, Margaret 36

Sappho 184
Satan 5, 16, 34, 56, 57, 61, 68, 148, 159, 175, 230, 231, 271
Saturday Review of Literature 27
Saturn 173
Schopenhauer, Arthur 27, 136
Schwob, Marcel 30
Scipio 234
"The Sea" 284
"Sea-Mania" 184
Seine 223, 259
Seitz, Don C. 33
Seven Seas Magazine 36, 234
Shakespeare, William 46, 63, 170, 183, 189, 199
"Shelley" 169
Shelley, Percy Bysshe 38, 62, 67, 168, 193, 265
"The Shrine in the Mist" 23, 76
Siberia 162, 224
Siegfried 154, 175
"Similes and a Query" 37, 257
Simplement Vagabondages 298
"Sleep" 177, 251
"The Sleeper" 53, 115, 301
The Smart Set 5
Smith, Clark Ashton 36
"Solitude" 30, 206
"Solitude" (Fr) 207
"Song of Songs" 230
"Song of Vengeance and Victory" 35
Sophocles 65, 67, 136
"Sorrow's Balm" 30, 203
"The Soul of It All" 256
"The Spear of the Great Spurning" 119
"The Specter Life" 50

318

Sphinx 79, 141, 152, 215, 258
Spinoza, Baruch 21, 45, 46, 64, 154, 306
St. Elmo 172
Sterling, George 24, 25
St. Helena 234
Stieglitz, Alfred 15, 16, 30
Stirner, Max 16, 17, 38
The St. Louis Post-Dispatch 27
"Strayling" 185
Stuck, Franz von 36
The Sublime Boy 24
"Sub Specie Eternitatis" 253
Sultan 224, 249, 263
sun 139, 142, 146, 151, 236, 244, 250, 266, 304
"Swinburne" 188
Swinburne, Algernon Charles 69, 188
Symbolism 16, 31
"The Syncopated Spinner" 93
Syria 64

"Tamar" 63, 65, 66, 67
Tantalus 195
"Tantara! Tantaro!" 74
Temple of Pain 51, 81
Thaïs 143
The Aristocrat 29
"The-Circle-That-Looks-Like-A-Line" 79
"The Coast-Range Christ" 63, 66
"The Coming Slavery" 41
"The Dynasts" 64
The Fra 15
"The Haunted House" 28
"The Suicide" 25
"The Thief" 187
Thor 169, 277

Thoreau, Henry David 46
"Threshold" 283
Thus Spake Zarathustra 52, 69
"Times Schoolhouse" 37
Titan 35, 51, 150, 162, 198, 223, 224, 274, 284
Titania 277, 289
Titian 270
"To a Great American" 266
"To Benjamin DeCasseres" 6, 18
"To Emile Verhaeren" 35, 223
"The Tongueless One" 75
Torquemada 33, 222, 228
"To the Old Soak" 39, 290
"The Tower Beyond Tragedy" 63, 67
"The Tragic Bluffer" 174
The Triumph of Life 38
Trotsky, Leon 15
"The Truant" 106
Tzgaines 211

"The Ultimate" 114
Ultima Thule 191
Unamuno, Miguel de 45, 46
"The Undying Flame" 254
University of Chicago 18, 29
"Unwithered" 125
"Uprendered" 124
Uriah 226

Valhalla 58, 193, 235, 274
Valkyrie 175, 184, 193, 231, 289
"The Vampire" 37, 265
Vampire 265
Vanity Fair 5
Var 259
"Variations on an Old Theme" 260
"The Vat" 189

Vautrin 68
Vedanta 52
Venus 140, 147, 274
Verdun 144, 168, 259
Verhaeren, Emile 35, 223
vers libre 17, 28, 55
"Vers Libre" 28, 179
"Vicariously" 39, 280
Victory 215, 223
Viereck, George Sylvester 30
"The Vigil" 49, 98
Virginia 29
"Vision" 287
"The Vision Malefic" 83
von Hartmann, Eduard.
    See Hartmann, Eduard
    von
von Stuck, Franz. *See* Stuck,
    Franz von
Vulcan 16, 35, 48, 245

Wagner, Richard 67, 265
Wagstaff, Blanche Shoemaker
    18, 19
"Waiting" 126
"Walter" 160
The Washington News Letter 30
The Washington Times 243, 245,
    248, 249, 250, 252, 253,
    254, 255, 256, 257
"The Watcher" 95
Waterloo 168
"The Way Out: Bio" 110
Weber, Max 36
Webster's Unabridged Dictionary
    38
Weimar 88
Wells, H. G. 63
Wessex 62
"West Point" 208

Whitechapel 62
White Temple 92
Whitman, Walt 21, 30, 36, 39,
    63, 70, 266, 284
Wilde, Oscar 36
Wilmarth Publishing 21
The Wilmington Dispatch 37,
    261
Wilson, Woodrow 64
"Wind" 277
"The Wisdom of Gautama" 30,
    204
Wolff, Adolf 30, 36
"The Women at Point Sur" 63,
    67, 68
Wood, Clement 38
The Works of Benjamin De-
    Casseres 28
Wotan 143
"W.S.: 1616-1916" 227

Zarathustra 49, 68, 186
Zayas, Marius de 20, 23
Zeus 198

Books and Booklets

Anathema!: Litanies Of Negation
ISBN: 978-0988553620

The Sublime Boy (by Walter DeCasseres)
ISBN: 978-0988553675

New York Is Hell: Thinking and Drinking in the Beautiful Beast
ISBN: 978-0988553606

Benjamin DeCasseres Ephemera (Ltd.ed./66) | SA1025

Fantasia Impromptu & Finis
ISBN: 978-0988553668

"*To Hell With DeCasseres!*" | SA1081

The Thinker (Ltd.ed./23)

Fulminations: Caustic, Cosmic, Capricious
ISBN: 978-1943687152

The Boy of Bethlehem (by Bio DeCasseres) (Ltd.ed./33) | SA1131

Spinoza: Liberator Of God And Man & Against The Rabbis
ISBN: 978-6976196152

Ink-Stained Imp and The Pugilist Painter (Ltd.ed./66) | SA1155

The Individualist (Ltd.ed./66) | SA1180

The Works Of Benjamin DeCasseres Vol. 1 | SA1200

The Works Of Benjamin DeCasseres Vol. 2 | SA1201

The Works Of Benjamin DeCasseres Vol. 3 | SA1202

Parents: What are they Good For? | SA1252
ISBN: 978-1735643861

An American Wrestles With God (Ltd.ed./66) | SA1300

Imp: The Collected Poetry Of Benjamin DeCasseres
ISBN: 978-1943687404

The Jingo Poems (Ltd.ed./33) | SA1313

A title followed by "SA" with a number designates it as an issue of the multi-format journal *Stand Alone*.

Writing by and about Benjamin DeCasseres is featured in most issues of *Der Geist: The Journal of Egoism from 1845 to 1945*.

STANDARD FREETHOUGHT WORKS

BANNER OF THE ANTICHRIST—*Enzo Martucci*	$18
BATTLE HYMNS OF TOIL & QUIVARA—*Covington Hall*	$15
BLOOD & VOLTS—*Th. Metzger*	$16
COLLECTED WRITINGS OF RENZO NOVATORE—*Wolfi Landstreicher (trans.)*	$15
CONFESSIONS OF A FAILED EGOIST—*Trevor Blake*	$10
HOMO 99 AND 44/100 NONSAPIENS—*Gerald B. Lorentz*	$18
MIGHT IS RIGHT: THE AUTHORITATIVE EDITION—*Ragnar Redbeard*	$20
MIGHT IS RIGHT: 1927 FACSIMILE EDITION—*Ragnar Redbeard*	$16
MIGHT IS RIGHT: THE REBEL POETRY OF—*Covington Hall*	$9
THE OCCULT TECHNOLOGY OF POWER—*The Transcriber*	$8
THE PHILOSOPHICAL WRITINGS OF EDGAR SALTUS—*Edgar Saltus*	$18
THE RADICAL BOOK SHOP OF CHICAGO—*Kevin I. Slaughter*	$16
THE RED SECT—*Enzo Martucci*	$16
RIVAL CAESARS: A ROMANCE...—*Ragnar Redbeard*	$20
THE SATANIC SCRIPTURES—*Peter H. Gilmore*	$17
SORCERIES AND SCANDALS OF SATAN—*Henry M. Tichenor*	$15
THIS UGLY CIVILIZATION—*Ralph Borsodi*	$20

BENJAMIN DeCASSERES SERIES:

ANATHEMA! LITANIES OF NEGATION	$10
FANTASIA IMPROMPTU & FINIS	$16
FULMINATIONS: CAUSTIC, COSMIC, CAPRICIOUS	$16
IMP: THE COLLECTED POETRY OF BENJAMIN DeCASSERES	$18
THE JINGO POEMS (Booklet)	$5
NEW YORK IS HELL: THINKING AND DRINKING IN THE BEAUTIFUL BEAST	$18
SPINOZA: LIBERATOR OF GOD AND MAN & AGAINST THE RABBIS	$15
THE BOY OF BETHLEHEM—*Bio DeCasseres* (Hardbound)	$23
THE SUBLIME BOY—*Walter DeCasseres*	$7

THE PORTABLE L.A.ROLLINS SERIES:

THE MYTH OF NATURAL RIGHTS	$15
LUCIFER'S LEXICON	$15
OUTLAW HISTORY	$15

PAMPHLETS

BOVARYSM: THE ART-PHILOSOPHY OF JULES DE GAULTIER—*Wilmot E. Ellis*	$4
IMMORALITY AS A PHILOSOPHIC PRINCIPLE—*Paul Carus*	$5
MAX STIRNER AND THE PHILOSOPHY OF THE INDIVIDUAL—*Leo Markun*	$8
THE NIETZSCHE MOVEMENT IN ENGLAND—*Oscar Levy*	$2
ON ACTIVE SERVICE—*J.A.Andrews*	$4
PRIMITIVES: POEMS AND WOODCUTS—*Max Weber*	$6
THE RIP-SAW MOTHER GOOSE—*Henry Tichenor*	$4
SOCIALISM: AN ACTUAL EXPERIMENT—*Stewart Grahame*	$4

UNDERWORLD AMUSEMENTS
444 MARYLAND AVE. #7940   ESSEX, MD 21221

For postage add $4 for the first item, $1 for each additional.

www.ingramcontent.com/pod-product-compliance
Lightning Source LLC
Chambersburg PA
CBHW060514080526
44586CB00012B/479